101 Ways to Participate in Having a World that Works for Everyone

101 Ways to Participate in Having a World that Works for Everyone

◆

So, What are You Going to do about it?

Compiled by Lyle Smith

Writer's Showcase
New York Lincoln Shanghai

101 Ways to Participate in Having a World that Works for Everyone
So, What are You Going to do about it?

Writer's Showcase
an imprint of iUniverse, Inc.

For information address:
iUniverse, Inc.
2021 Pine Lake Road, Suite 100
Lincoln, NE 68512
www.iuniverse.com

ISBN: 0-595-26472-7

Printed in the United States of America

Contents

Section III Support Efforts Focused on Particular Important Issues 55

Preface

September 11th, 2001. I'm sure you remember where you were and what you were doing. I was in Park City, Utah, helping my son, Scott, with his painting business. We had just come from the paint store where we picked up supplies and were on the way to a job site when his cell phone rang. My wife, at work in Chicago, called. "Do you guys know what happened?" We were clueless. After she told us about the plane that had crashed into one of the twin towers in New York City we dashed to Scott's condo and turned on the TV. We were then glued to it for hours!

"So, *do* something about it!"

Haven't you wanted to say that to someone who was complaining about a situation? Maybe even to yourself?

One Man's Promise

"I promise a world of economic freedom for all, beyond the end of hunger, by 2020."
This promise comes from the life I have lived so far, and from a desire to participate in the improvement of the planet while I'm here. The promise also comes from nothing. I make this promise as a platform from which to live the rest of my life.

This book comes from my promise and is offered as a guide or a push to get more involved than you are. If we all step up our commitment to the planet as our collective home, we can indeed make it a better place.

Buckminster Fuller (**www.bfi.org**) made a commitment to see what one man could do for the planet if he dedicated himself to that purpose. He left a legacy of great ideas/patents and inspiration to those of us who are alive to carry on the work of making the planet a better place for our having enjoyed it for our lifetime.

Smallpox is gone! Polio is nearly gone! We know we can achieve great goals with the alignment of our will and resources. Let's get it done! This book is my shot at jostling us into alignment, and encouraging one more human being to line up on this task.

This book is *not* about supporting charities. This book is about taking part in the solution. This book is about doing something and, for some of us, doing something more. Should we support charities? Yes, supporting charities is one of the obvious and relatively easy things to do. However, some of the hard things to do are crucial too. See Number 82.

Can we do it? Hell, yes!
How do I know? Because human beings are more powerful than we know—when we align and take on a vision—anything can be done!
Carpe diem!

May I, may you, may we
not die unlived lives.
May none of us live in fear
of falling or catching fire.
May we choose to inhabit our days,
to allow our living to open us,
to make us less afraid,
more accessible,
to loosen our hearts
until they become wings,
torches, promises.
May each of us choose to risk our significance,
to live so that which comes to us as seen
goes to the next as blossom
and that which comes to us as blossom
goes on as fruit.

Dawna Markova

Make today count!

Thanks for tuning in.
Lyle

101 ways to participate:

So, look through this list and pick something that appeals to you. Or, pick something that you have an interest in. Pick something! Do something! **Action** is what makes a difference in the world and will make it work for all of us.

By the way (about donating)

In a recent (mid-2001) *Reader's Digest* I ran across this bit of information:

Melinda and Bill Gates gave $5 billion to charity last year (2000).

But the super-rich are not the only ones opening their wallets. Independent Sector reports 70% of American households make donations to charity, averaging a total of $1075 per year.

Total given	$203 billion
Corporations	$ 11 billion
Foundations	$ 25 billion
Individuals	$152 billion

% of income to charity:	
Average contributor	2.1%
College graduates	2.0
Income below $10,000	5.3
Income over $100,000	2.2
Churchgoers	2.3
Non-churchgoers	1.3
Retirees	2.5

Choosing an Organization to Support

One of the key questions people ask when they are choosing from among the many, many opportunities to donate their money is what percentage of the funds get to the bottom line of the cause. There is not always a simple answer or analysis of where the money goes. For most organizations a net of around 80% of the funds going to the intended cause is viewed as good. That is, if no more than 20% of donated or collected funds are spend on administrative and fundraising expenses, we usually consider that the organization is making effective use of the funds raised. All public organizations are required to report their financials and from the web sites cited throughout this book there is usually a pointer to how their annual report can be obtained. When in doubt, check it out!

Remember, however, supporting organizations is one of many ways to participate in the solution to having a world that works for everyone. It is probably the easiest way for many of us and clearly as I collected items for this book such were most of the items I collected. However, take on other issues as you are so moved. See, for example, item number 82, **Listen** to People

Note about how this book was prepared

Over a period of about two years I collected items that came in my mailbox such as solicitations from charities, I noticed what people are doing in the world as I read news magazines, and I kept in the forefront of my thinking the collection of possible items to be included in this book. My file grew and grew and it seemed that as I made donations to those who solicited me through the mail my mailbox grew fuller. One day I wrote checks to about 30 different organizations that appear in this book Since then I have decided to concentrate our family's donations to the organizations I consider to be involved in "trimtab" activities. Now, the number of donations has gone down considerably but the amounts have gone up.

For many of the items in this book there is a web site maintained by the organization of note. I have frequently copied some information from the web site to make it easy to read about what they are doing without going to the website itself. I have contacted each web site so used for permission to copy from their site and in all cases such permission has been granted. I have also copied information from brochures published by some of the organizations and have also written to ask for permission to copy them also. Permission has been given in all cases.

Material from web sites often includes what looks like links to other sites but this book does not include the ability to do such linking. If you go to the actual web site, of course, you can click on the links successfully. I certainly recommend that you go to the actual web site for the organizations that you are interested in supporting. That is why I have included the web site *url* in every case where one is available.

Carpe Diem! *Do* **something about it!**

Section I
Support Key Organizations—Trimtabs, that have a greater influence than it might seem at first.

1.—The Hunger Project and "A Night for a Dream" www.thp.org

This, my friends, is one of my favorites. The Hunger Project gets a mention in our will. The Hunger Project gets 50% of any net proceeds from this book. The Hunger Project also gets the most space (second only to #99, the Earth Charter) in this book. All this **is** worth looking at either here or on the web site.

The Hunger Project began in 1977 with a launching event in October. I attended a satellite broadcast of the opening of the Hunger Project, and was an active participant from 1977 on. One of the initial activities carried out by the Hunger Project was to enroll people in the idea that ending hunger was an idea whose time had come. We had enrollment cards we asked folks to fill out and sign. On the card they would pick their type of participation in the Hunger Project. Participation opportunities ranged from active involvement in the enrollment activities, to donating money, to creating one's own form of participation. Millions were enrolled, and for a few years they were sent a newsletter every quarter or so. My sons were enrolled too and they would bring home signed cards from their classmates at school.

Ever since 1977 The Hunger Project has been active in bringing about the political will needed to end hunger on this planet. Along the way, the actor, Raul Julia, became involved with the Hunger Project and was a huge supporter. After he died, an annual event in his honor has been held by the Hunger Project to honor Raul's efforts and to continue them with a special celebration and fund raising event. The fifth such event, "A Night for a Dream" was held in San Juan, Puerto Rico on the 10th of March, 2001. **www.thp.org**

From the web site:

The Hunger Project is a strategic organization and global movement committed to the sustainable end of world hunger.

In Africa, Asia and Latin America, we empower local people to create lasting society-wide progress in health, education, nutrition and family incomes. We apply a two-prong strategy: mobilizing grassroots self-reliant action, and mobilizing local leadership to clear away obstacles to enable grassroots action to succeed.

Our highest priority is the empowerment of women. Women bear primary responsibility for family health, education and nutrition—yet, by tradition, culture and law they are denied the means, information and freedom of action to fulfill their responsibility. The Hunger Project is committed to transforming this condition.

Unleashing the Human Spirit

- *Principles and Methodology of The Hunger Project*

- *Effective Strategy and Action for a Future Free from Hunger*

15 April 1996, Updated November 1997
Confronting the Challenge of Ending Hunger

- **Hunger persists:** Each and every day, 24,000 people die as a consequence of chronic, persistent hunger. Between 750 million to 1 billion people live in conditions of poverty so severe that they are unable to obtain enough food to meet their daily requirements. This is not the kind of hunger that makes headlines, as in a famine, but a silent holocaust that continues day after day, month after month.

- **Hunger can be ended:** This waste of human lives is all the more tragic in that it can be ended. The world produces more than enough food for everyone and, if we act wisely, can continue to do so for future generations. The world community possesses the financial and technical resources necessary to end hunger.

- **The world has committed itself to this goal**. At the 1990 World Summit for Children and at a series of global conferences, including the Earth Summit in Rio, the Population Conference in Cairo, the Social Development Summit in Copenhagen and the Women's Conference in Beijing, the world community has committed itself time and again to meeting a series of goals by the year 2000 that would result in the end of hunger on our planet.

- **A moral imperative/a practical necessity.** These conferences have stressed that ending hunger is not only a moral imperative, but a practical necessity. Ending hunger is central to resolving an entire nexus of issues, such as population growth, civil unrest and environmental destruction, which will increasingly threaten the quality of life for everyone.

- **A human issue.** Today, ending hunger is not primarily a technical or a production issue, it is a *human* issue. Hunger persists because we, as human beings, have failed to organize our societies in ways that assure every person the chance to live a healthy and productive life.

- **Limits to the conventional approach.** Ending hunger is a highly complex challenge. It is increasingly clear that charitable responses and traditional bureaucratic programs, as useful as they may be, are insufficient to carry the day. More importantly, people increasingly recognize that conventional approaches are based on a *framework of thinking* that is inconsistent with what actually must be done to achieve the end of hunger on a sustainable basis.

- **The commitment of The Hunger Project:** The Hunger Project is committed to the *end* of hunger. This means that we are committed to empowering people to create permanent, society-wide solutions to the problem, and not content ourselves with charitable actions that only benefit a few. We are committed to identifying and utilizing an accurate framework of thinking, and pioneering strategies and actions that will enable humanity to create a new future—a future free from hunger.

The Need for a New Set of Principles

- The Hunger Project believes that the strategies and actions required to end hunger must emanate from a new set of principles. These principles are derived from an authentic **confrontation with the commitment to ending hunger**, and from a **deeper examination of what it means to be human.**

- **Discovered in action:** The principles of The Hunger Project are not created in a philosophical vacuum and then applied. They evolve and are refined in the action itself. The formulation of our principles changes as our experience grows. In this way, there is no room for arrogance. On the contrary, the work of ending hunger is a rigorous teacher of a complex subject, constantly requiring a spirit of humility and openness to discovery.

The Principles of The Hunger Project:
Who We Are as Human Beings

The persistence of hunger is a human issue. Therefore, the principles of The Hunger Project begin with the recognition of two essential elements of what it means to be human.

- **The human spirit:** The Hunger Project recognizes that in addition to survival needs, every human being has a fundamental need to lead a life of dignity, meaning and purpose—to know that our lives make a difference.

- **Interconnectedness:** Our actions are shaped by and affect all other people and our natural environment. Our responsibility extends beyond our immediate lives and families to the entire human family. Issues of hunger and poverty are not problems of one country or another but are global issues, and we must solve them as global citizens.

The Principles of The Hunger Project:
Creating a New Future

Ending hunger requires a true break with the status quo. It will not happen in the course of "business as usual." To resolve humanity's oldest and most pernicious problem requires four essential ingredients:

- **Vision**: Given who we are as human beings, what is critical to our progress is vision—seeing a future that can be achieved and is worth achieving. The vision that calls forth The Hunger Project is a sustainable future for humanity, a future in which all people have the opportunity to live healthy and productive lives in harmony with nature. We call this "the end of hunger."

- **Commitment:** Commitment is what allows individuals to encounter obstacles, frustrations and failures on the pathway to achievement and still keep going. It is increasingly clear that achieving the future we envision will not just happen. It must be made to happen, and this will require extraordinary commitment. Calling forth that commitment, and keeping it focused and sustained to fulfill the vision, is a vital responsibility of The Hunger Project.

- **Leadership:** Leadership is critical to every great human achievement. Ending hunger requires committed leadership at all levels of society—from the village to the district, state, nation and the international community—that can call forth vision and commitment, and mobilize people to take effective action.

- **Strategy and Action:** Meeting a challenge as complex and daunting as hunger in a world of finite resources requires brilliant strategy and high-leverage action. It requires inquiry, analysis and allocation of resources consistent with achieving the goal. Every action must be designed to take a quantum leap forward towards the goal. There must also be extraordinary flexibility of action. One must move down a pathway with sufficient intentionality to make progress, yet be willing at every moment to let go of one approach to take a better pathway.

The Principles of The Hunger Project:
A Paradigm for Success

The Hunger Project recognizes that creating truly effective strategies and actions for the end of hunger requires a new framework of thinking, that is, a new paradigm—a paradigm consistent with the end of hunger. The key elements of that new paradigm are

- **Self-reliance:** Conventional approaches have treated hungry people as the problem instead of the solution, as beneficiaries rather than the primary actors, working for their own self-reliance. All individuals have the right and the responsibility to be the authors of their own lives and their own development. The work of ending hunger must build from people's own creativity—their own skills, resources and decision making.

- **Enabling Environment:** People's ability to express their self-reliance is a function of the opportunities provided by the society. The work of ending hunger is therefore not feeding people. It is the work of creating an enabling environment in which people have the opportunity and empowerment they need to build lives of self-reliance.

- **Empowerment of women**: Women and girls are the most affected by hunger and poverty. Traditionally, women bear the primary responsibilities in the most relevant areas—food production, nutrition, family planning, primary health and education. Yet most development inputs continue to go to men. A central component of effective strategy must be the empowerment of women in ways that enable her to achieve improvements in all key areas that affect their lives and those of their families.

- **Global responsibility, partnership and investment:** Hunger is a global issue. All of us have the responsibility to stand in partnership with hungry people, committed to their success. The achievement of this goal represents a new future, not only for those who are hungry but for all people. Realizing this new future for all humanity requires investment, not charity.

The Campaign to End Hunger

- **Not a program, but a phenomenon:** The work of ending hunger cannot be accomplished by any one organization, or even any conceivable network of organizations. The end of hunger will not be a series of well-managed projects. It will be achieved through millions of actions, most of which will never be recognized, and will certainly not be monitored and measured.

- The end of hunger will be a *phenomenon*—an unleashing of the creativity and productivity of hundreds of millions of hungry people, and hundreds of thousands of effective strategies and actions that create the enabling environment for them to succeed.

- **Catalyzing that phenomenon:** The phenomenon of strategy and action will not happen on its own. Individuals must take responsibility for making it happen.

- **A movement, not an organization:** For this reason, The Hunger Project can never be accurately thought of as merely an organization. It must be thought of as a *movement*, a campaign of individuals and organizations committed to taking strategic action to mobilize self-reliant development and transform the policy environment at every level so that people can succeed.

- **Galvanizing the campaign at every level of society:** The campaign for ending hunger starts with the creativity of hungry people—respecting them as the primary authors and actors of the work to end hunger, awakening them to a possibility for a better life, and working to clear away the obstacles to the success of their self-reliant action.

- Building upon the self-reliant efforts of hungry people, the campaign to end hunger must take action at every level of society—from the local level up to the national government, and to the level of the international community.

Strategic Planning-in-Action—a Methodology for Accomplishment, Focus and Breakthrough

To meet the challenge of ending hunger requires a methodology that will break up old patterns of action, that will foster new ways of thinking and empower people to achieve concrete break-throughs in health, education, nutrition, food production, incomes and the empowerment of women.

The methodology developed by The Hunger Project to achieve this is called **strategic planning-in-action**. Wherever we work, from the villages to the highest policy levels, we apply this methodology:

- **Mobilize and empower committed indigenous leadership**: The first step in our work is always to enlist the leadership of individuals of great commitment, complete integrity and the stature to access anyone in society necessary to ending hunger. Leadership for action in a village must come from that village; leadership for action in a nation must come from that nation. These individuals must become completely clear about and committed to utilizing the principles and methodology of The Hunger Project.

- **Bring together all sectors of society:** Ending hunger cannot be accomplished by government alone. We bring together leadership from all key sectors—business, academia, NGOs and government agencies—forming councils to create and lead our strategies in co-equal partnership.

- **Build a shared understanding:** For people to work together effectively, they must achieve a comprehensive shared understanding of the prevailing conditions, the effectiveness of existing programs and the priority areas where action is required. Bringing all the information together, and making it clear, finite and confrontable, has been one of the most empowering contributions of The Hunger Project since its inception.

- **Commit to achieving a strategic intent:** Individuals working with The Hunger Project must develop a powerfully articulated, unifying and achievable vision—a strategic intent—and clear strategic objectives appropriate to solving the problem, society-wide. We must never be content with helping a few, but rather commit ourselves to transforming conditions throughout society so that *all* people can build lives free from hunger.

- **Commit to playing a strategic, catalytic role:** Once people are committed to actually achieving the goal, they must then recognize the possibility of taking catalytic, high-leverage action that can affect the "big picture"—breaking bottlenecks to progress, improving existing programs, mobilizing and making better use of resources, effecting structural changes in society that can unleash the creativity and productivity of hungry people.

- **Identify what's missing:** Our work is always guided by the question, What's missing? What, if provided, would allow for a breakthrough? This is very different, and far more powerful, than the more common questions, What's wrong? Why isn't it working? These latter questions tend to call forth blame and paralysis, not action and cooperation. The Hunger Project respects the work of other organizations—by focusing on what's missing, we avoid duplicating work being done by others.

- **Take immediate action** to catalyze "what's missing" being provided. Take action first where it can succeed and produce near-term results.

- **Create a momentum of accomplishment:** One must constantly assess and sharpen the strategy. Each accomplishment gives a new landscape: new leadership, new obstacles, and new openings for catalytic action. Each failure can lead to a deeper understanding of the nature of the challenge. Creating and sustaining this campaign men-

tality and style of working is crucial to breaking the mind-set of res-
ignation and unleashing the human spirit.

Creating a World Free from Hunger

- One of the failures of development has been the belief that the way
  to end hunger is to find a workable solution and replicate it. This
  fails because the **source of the success is the human creativity** that
  resulted in the solution, not the solution itself.

- **Extend the process, don't replicate the solution.** Ending hunger
  will be achieved by extending the process of human empowerment,
  not by finding a model that works and replicating it.

- In every village where hunger persists, human beings must be
  empowered to discover their own vision, express their own leadership, and create their own solutions and work together to achieve
  their own success. At every level of society, the commitment of government officers, researchers, business people and citizen activists
  must be mobilized into a common front, transforming policies and
  structures so that all people have the chance to lead healthy and productive lives.

- The principles and methodology of The Hunger Project are applica-
  ble at all levels of society. They are derived from what it means to be
  human, and designed to facilitate human beings working together
  effectively.

- Discovering, applying and mastering this approach—being a catalyst in the worldwide phenomenon of ending hunger—is perhaps
  the greatest opportunity of this generation. From this perspective,
  one discovers that ending hunger is not fundamentally a problem to
  be solved, but a profound opportunity for unleashing the human
  spirit.

THE HUNGER PROJECT, 15 East 26 *th* *Street, New York, NY*
10010 USA

2.—THE BUCKMINSTER FULLER INSTITUTE
WWW.BFI.ORG

The Buckminster Fuller Institute is keeping alive the ideas and concern for the welfare of the planet Earth that Bucky Fuller (R Buckminster Fuller (1895-1983)) spent most of his life addressing.

From the web site: www.bfi.org © 2002 Buckminster Fuller Institute

This site is devoted to advancing **Humanity's Option for Success**, inspired by the principles articulated by Buckminster Fuller. We hope to empower site visitors to see the big picture and exercise individual initiative. Everyone on board our Spaceship Earth can live abundantly and successfully on an ecologically sustainable basis. Humanity has the option to make it. We must choose it before it expires.

"Whether it is to be Utopia or Oblivion will be a touch-and-go relay race right up to the final moment."
—Buckminster Fuller 1980

On a personal note—It was in the late 1970's when I was employed at Northern Illinois University, probably 1978 or 1979 that Bucky Fuller was invited by a campus organization to come give a talk.
I knew of Bucky from my involvement in The Hunger Project (see # 1) and so was interested in hearing his talk. I don't recall his talk but I do recall getting in line to get his autograph after the presentation. I had cards for enrolling into The Hunger Project and thought myself very clever as I asked this famous man to sign on the back of a Hunger Project enrollment card. That was the first of, I think, three autographs I have obtained in my whole life. I have since lost that card, but it was a proud souvenir for some years.
After the events on September 11th, 2001, Bucky's words seem even more important than ever!

Here is information about a lecture series that Buckminster Fuller gave
in 1975.
From the web site: http://www.bfi.org/everything_i_know.htm© 2002 Buckminster Fuller Institute

Everything I Know by R. Buckminster Fuller
This transcription of 42 hours of lectures is available for sale as a transcript or as audio files online.
First Edition: Published by the Buckminster Fuller Institute
For information contact:
Buckminster Fuller Institute
111 N. Main Street
Sebastopol, CA 95472
Phone: 707-824-2242, Fax 707-824-2243
Email: **info@bfi.org**
All proceeds from the sale of this publication go directly to the Buckminster Fuller Institute to further their work.

Acknowledgments
We would like to gratefully acknowledge and thank JoAnne Ishimine whose care and dedication in transcribing the entire 42 hours of the Everything I Know series as a volunteer was an inspiration in getting this project off the ground. Her contribution is a striking example of what one individual can do, and in this project she has made a big difference. We would also like to acknowledge Ed Applewhite for his foresight and commitment in producing the outstanding outline which he prepared while in attendance at the lectures, and for which he has over the years allowed us to include as part of the Everything I Know publications. In addition we would like to thank dedicated volunteers Russell Chu, Jim Morrisett, Robert Orenstein and the many BFI staff members who assisted in various aspects of the preparation of materials.

Preface

During the last two weeks of January 1975 Buckminster Fuller gave an extraordinary series of lectures concerning his entire life's work. These thinking out loud lectures span 42 hours and examine in depth all of Fuller's major inventions and discoveries from the 1927 Dymaxion[a] house, car and bathroom, through the Wichita House, geodesic domes, and tensegrity structures, as well as the contents of Synergetics. Autobiographical in parts, Fuller recounts his own personal history in the context of the history of science and industrialization. The stories behind his Dymaxion[a] car, geodesic domes, World Game and integration of science and humanism are lucidly communicated with continuous reference to his synergetic geometry. Permeating the entire series is his unique comprehensive design approach to solving the problems of the world. Some of the topics Fuller covered in this wide ranging discourse include: architecture, design, philosophy, education, mathematics, geometry, cartography, economics, history, structure, industry, housing and engineering.

Study Buckminster Fuller's life and keep his vision alive.

Buckminster Fuller is listed first as the most influential futurist in the history of the world by professional futurists who were surveyed in a book published in 1996. The survey results are in an appendix to "The Encyclopedia of the Future", a 1,115 page two-volume tome published initially in 1996.
Bucky Fuller envisioned a World Game where individuals or teams would come together to compete, or cooperate to: "Make the world work, for 100% of humanity, in the shortest possible time, through spontaneous cooperation, without ecological offense or the disadvantage of anyone."

As mentioned above, there is an institute that carries on for Fuller since his death. Check out **www.bfi.org** The institute sent me the following paragraph that briefly describes them (Thanks Deborah).

Buckminster Fuller Institute
Committed to a successful and sustainable future for all humanity, the
Buckminster Fuller Institute (BFI) is a nonprofit organization inspired
by the Design Science principles pioneered by the late R. Buckminster
Fuller. BFI information resources and programs include: BFI.org, an
extensive web site on Fuller's life and work; EARTHscope (space-
shipearth.org), a web based "geo-story-telling" tool to depict critical
world trends; forums, lecture series, curriculum development, and
speaker referrals; member newsletter "Trimtab;" free monthly e-bulle-
tin; online store featuring Fuller's books and maps, videos and tapes.

Buckminster Fuller Institute
111 N. Main Street
Sebastopol, California 95472
707-824-2242; 800-967-6277
Website: **www.bfi.org** Email: **info@bfi.org**

And, don't miss the one man play presented by
Foghouse Productions
in association with ODAAT Productions
R. Buckminster Fuller:
THE HISTORY
(and Mystery)
OF THE UNIVERSE

Written and Directed by D.W. Jacobs
From the life, work and writings of R. Buckminster Fuller
Performed by Ron Campbell
For info and online tix go to www.foghouse.com

"Startlingly funny, intellectually stimulating and genuinely mov-
ing"
—Hurwitt, SF Examiner

"Inspiring and invigorating...it's hard to imagine a better one-man performance"
—LaSalle, SF Chronicle
SF CHRONICLE'S HIGHEST RATING!

"Hugely entertaining"
—Braunagel, LA Times

"SURGEON GENERAL'S WARNING: Caution, this play contains IDEAS!"
—Smith, San Diego Reader

3.—AIDSRIDE 2001 AND AIDSVACCINE RIDES—AIDS VACCINE RESEARCH

We recently received in the mail our invitation to get ready for 2001. AIDSRides have been taking place for several years now (the first ride was in California in 1994). Friends of ours got involved as van drivers on the "sweep team" for the 1999 Minneapolis to Chicago AIDSRide. They told us it was the most moving experience of their lives!
Their daughter was one of the riders, which only added to the experience. Her report was equally inspiring. We (my wife and I) had signed up to be on the sweep team in 2000 but other scheduled family activities took precedence. Our friends volunteered for the Alaska AIDSRide. They still rave about it!

These rides do much more than simply raise money to support those of us who have AIDS in our lives. The rides get people in action, inspire people, make people aware, AND raise money!

Now (January 2001) Diana and I have registered to be crew volunteers for the Montana AIDSVaccine Ride (July 30 through August 5, 2001)

And see **www.pallottateamworks.com**

When we returned from our Montana experience we sent the following email to our sponsors and friends and relatives.

**"How we spent our summer vacation (July 28-Aug 6, 2001)
Or
1025 bicycle riders, 565 miles, up and down mountains for 7 days!**

We did it! We flew to Missoula Montana, got ready to follow 1025 bicycle riders across the state to Billings, and started out early Monday morning on July 30th. There were about 300 of us volunteer crew members on a dozen or so different crews. Ours was the sweep team who rode in vans along the route, patrolling to pick up anyone needing assistance. There were a couple hundred or so various staff members working the ride too. It takes a lot of hands to make a moving tent city work as smoothly as this one did. Shower trucks, a huge dining tent, various other tents to set up each night and the 800 or so small, double occupancy tents for the riders and crew to sleep in each night! Diana and I enjoyed driving David's (another crew member—massage crew) Ford Excursion which was plenty big enough for us to sleep in each night so we could skip setting up our tent and taking it down each night (it rained at least twice—significantly!).

We met some wonderful people on the route as we got to pick some of the riders up and transport them to the next outpost. We would usually have them on board for 10 to 15 minutes. That was long enough in that **friendly, human kindness experiment**, environment that the ride was, to get to know each a little.

To those of you we picked up for a ride—thanks for choosing us!

Here is an example of what the environment created on the ride was like. On the sixth day of the ride (we did not rest on the seventh—but it was only about 55 miles for the riders!) I lost my wallet! It had in it all the usual credit cards, driver's license etc., and also over $300 in cash! Somehow I wasn't worried. I just knew someone would find it and turn it in intact. And they did! I do not even know who did it! Now, I have lost my wallet a couple times before in my life. It did not come back our there in the world we usually live in. The AIDS Vaccine Ride did indeed create a moving environment that exhibited a level of human kindness we do not usually experience.

And, in addition to the successful experiment in human kindness, each of the 1025 riders raised over $3,400 in pledges. After the expenses of the ride (e.g. that Ford Excursion gave us about 13 miles to the gallon, and there were a lot of portapotties to be moved each day!), there will be millions of dollars going directly to the three cooperating AIDS Vaccine research centers that were designated as the recipients of the money.

As I mentioned to some of the riders we picked up in our "sweep" van, I am working on a book titled "So, What Are You Going To Do About It?" (Or "101 ways to Participate in making the World Work"). Participating in the Montana AIDS Vaccine Ride is certainly one of the 101 ways to make the world work.

Congratulation to all the riders, the crew members and the staff for a successful event!

For anyone reading this that wasn't on the ride—go to **www. pallottateamworks.com** for details! And **THANKS to you who sponsored us as crew members!**

So, do something about our world! I know, you already are—what else can you do?

Thanks a lot,
Yours, **for a world that works,**
   Lyle & Diana   8/10/01 dsslbs@aol.com"

2002 AIDS Vaccine Ride

After all that we then decided to actually participate in the 2002 AIDS Vaccine Ride from Amsterdam to Paris in Europe (June 30 through July 6). We bought bicycles, put in some long training rides, got involved in fundraising, and did the ride. Here is a brief report that we sent to those who sponsored us..

"We've been back from our AIDS Vaccine ride for a while now. We had an incredible journey.

The ride accomplishes three things. It raises money for AIDS Vaccine Research, builds awareness of the AIDS pandemic, and proves to the participants that they can go beyond the limitations they have set for themselves.

The challenges of the ride exceeded our expectations—or at least our capabilities! And having said that, we did far better than we thought we would. We rode 400 of the 540 very hilly, very rainy, very challenging miles. The weather presented its own unique challenges. A rainy weather front had settled over our ride and we dealt with rain every day except two, and rain every night except one. In addition the strong head winds kept us in lower gears constantly.

There were many rewards along the way. One day as we were stopped along the route a Frenchman who was mowing the other side of the road, stopped his work to cross the road and shake our hands to acknowledge what we were doing. Another Frenchman took Diana and two other gals to buy warm dry clothes. Other times we were cheered on by local people as we rode through their towns.

The 3rd objective of the ride is to raise money and we want to thank you for your support. As the AIDS story unfolds it becomes clear that America and Europe must play a large role in the end of AIDS. The numbers of infections and deaths continue to grow and we are often at a loss as to what we as individuals can do. You are an individual who did something. Your action of donating money raised awareness surrounding HIV/AIDS, contributed financially to AIDS Vaccine Research, and challenged us to see beyond the limits we had placed on ourselves (who knows what we'll take on next).

We thank you for your support.

For a world without AIDS,
Lyle & Diana"

Unfortunately, since the ride (as of September 2002), Pallotta Teamworks has encountered some unfavorable press, some rides with unexpectedly low net returns to the end recipients of the fundraising efforts of participants and the organization has closed its California office. Time will tell the next chapter of Pallotta Teamworks' efforts.

Start a Foundation—fund more research

As a consequence of our participation in the Vaccine ride, and the fundraising efforts we took on, we formed a Private Foundation called "For Global Progress, NFP" that we are using to continue to raise money for AIDS Vaccine Research. We plan two major fundraisers each year. Our initial goal was to raise $100,000. So far we have raised over $20,000.

To donate, send a check (or your name, address and credit card information Visa, M/C, or AmExpress) to:

For Global Progress
c/o M. Junius
7421 Isham
Chicago, IL 60631

The mission of "For Global Progress" is:

For Global Progress, NFP is a private not for profit foundation that promotes a world that works for everyone.

The foundation funds projects that forward progress on current world conditions.

Initially, the foundation is raising money directed towards AIDS vaccine research.

Section II
Support Organizations involved in World Wide Economic Bootstrapping

4.—SUPPORT CHILDREACH (PLAN INTERNATIONAL) WITH YOUR CONTRIBUTIONS
WWW.CHILDREACH.ORG

Several years ago my stepdaughter, a freshman in college at the University of Wisconsin in Madison, told us she was sponsoring a child in Africa. If she could come up with $22 each month for a child she had never met, couldn't her mother and I at least do the same? We took on sponsoring one child about 14 years ago. Since then I have found out a lot more about what Childreach does with the $22 and we now sponsor five children in various African countries. The money goes to community projects that support the improvement of the education and economics of the community. The connection with the children is a communication that sometimes continues beyond the program. Childreach also gets involved in disaster assistance and cooperates with the other NGO's in the areas they work. Childreach applies its efforts where they are most needed. For example, in Costa Rica, a democratic country with a large middle class population, the economy is in pretty good shape and Childreach is not engaged. Costa Rica's neighbors, however, are not in as good shape and we have, for example, sponsored a young lad in Honduras. Check 'em out! **www.childreach.org**

Every month or so we get letters and drawings from the sponsored children. It is like getting letters and drawings from one's grandchildren (in our case). And, every month or two I write a letter to the children we sponsor. Since we have five, I usually write a letter for all of them on my computer, print five copies and personalize each with the name of the individual children. I think if you carefully examine the many organizations that support developing countries in ways similar to Childreach, you will find this organization to be at least among the best around, and in any way you would measure the best.

News flash! Just recently (September 2002) we received a letter from Childreach to tell us that one of our foster children, a girl in Kenya, was "graduating" from the program and we could no longer sponsor her. Now, we are familiar with the fact that children who turn 18 years old are no longer eligible. This time, however, it was due to the village having become self sufficient! That, obviously, is the goal of the program. And it is working!

From the web site:

How We Help

"The child is at the center of everything we do."

Plan International is a child-centered organization that works at the grassroots level with children, their families and their communities. The ultimate objective of our work is to make lasting improvements in the lives of deprived children.

We achieve this by actively involving the children in all aspects of our development programs. Projects are planned, implemented, and their results are evaluated at the level of the child. Families and communities contribute as much as they can of their time, labor, and their funds—a value that can amount to more than half of project costs.

This child-centered approach to working with children demands new thinking. By designing programs at the level of the child, we can better see the complex web of causes and effects that impacts a child's life, and respond with programs in five interrelated areas of work, called Domains—Growing Up Healthy, Learning, Habitat, Livelihood and Building Relationships.

Domains define the scope of our work, what we try to achieve in our programs. Each Domain in every program location has a goal, a number of strategic objectives, and a set of impact indicators, against which we can measure the effectiveness of our programs in improving the well being of children.

What Makes Childreach Different

We are private:
Childreach is supported primarily by individual sponsors. Less than 17 percent of our total funding is from government or multilateral grants. Our private funding base keeps us free to focus on sponsored children and their families, and it means that we are responsible first to our individual donors and our mission to serve children.

We Are Non-Sectarian:
Childreach, with Plan International, is the largest non-sectarian sponsorship organization in the world. We do not impose religious values on the children and families we serve. We respect the diversity of religions and cultures of our program participants and do not seek to impose our own.

Our Programs Are Personal:
Plan International's field programs are tailor-made to help each sponsored child and family meet their basic needs, improve their economic and social conditions, and increase their ability to contribute to their societies. Personal sponsorship not only provides the reliable base of support necessary to sustain long-term programs; it also permits individual Americans to take a personal stake in the future of our world, with a personal connection to one of its neediest children.

We Are Committed to Building Relationships:
Childreach emphasizes quality communications between people in the U.S. and developing countries as an integral part of the development process. Our communications program has the specific goals of accountability to donors; linkage between sponsors and enrolled children and families; and development education.

We Are Accountable:

We have a policy and practice of accountability and openness. We observe a code of ethics and a code of conduct. We publish an annual report containing an audited financial statement. We encourage our sponsors to visit our programs overseas, to meet the children and families they are helping, and to observe the impact of their assistance firsthand.

5.—Support Oxfam
WWW.OXFAMAMERICA.ORG

Oxfam America seeks lasting solutions to poverty and social and economic injustice around the world. Oxfam knows that poverty and hunger are preventable problems and they seek ways to eliminate the root causes of inequities by working in partnership with grassroots organizations promoting sustainable development. Also, the organization advocates for policy change and offers educational opportunities for the public to become informed and involved in world affairs and development issues. Oxfam America is a member of Oxfam International, which comprises 11 autonomous Oxfams around the world. Oxfam is privately funded and nonsectarian.

How many Oxfams will we need to get this job (eliminating hunger and poverty) done?

From the web site:

What is Oxfam America?

Oxfam America invests privately raised funds and technical expertise in local organizations around the world that hold promise in their efforts to help poor people move out of poverty. These projects are characterized by what we call partnerships with these local organizations—a unique and highly successful approach that ensures lasting change. At Oxfam, we listen to our partners as they describe local needs, and we work together with them to find ways to help their communities prosper in their livelihoods and organize their communities for economic stability and democratic opportunity.

Oxfam is driven by a concern for social and economic justice. We have learned, after 30 years in our work, that poverty is not inevitable. It is the consequence of social and institutional inequities, economic exploitation, and unfair distribution of resources. Much of our work—in communities and as advocates with governments and decision-makers—is to identify and understand these barriers to equality and work together with our partners toward their eradication.

Oxfam is committed to long-term relationships in search of lasting solutions to hunger, poverty, and social inequities. We are equally dedicated to educating the public—in all quarters of the world—on the realities of poverty and on the universal obligation we have to establish a future that is equitable, environmentally sustainable, and respectful of the rights of all peoples.

The Oxfam Mission:

> Oxfam America is dedicated to creating lasting solutions to hunger, poverty, and social injustice through long-term partnerships with poor communities around the world. As a privately funded organization, we can speak with conviction and integrity as we challenge the structural barriers that foster conflict and human suffering and limit people from gaining the skills, resources, and power to become self-sufficient.

Our Vision:

Oxfam America envisions a world in which all people shall one day know freedom—freedom to achieve their fullest potential and to live secure from the dangers of hunger, deprivation, and oppression—through the creation of a global movement for economic and social justice.

Our Values:

To create lasting solutions to hunger, poverty, and injustice, Oxfam America believes:

- In the essential dignity of all peoples and their right to pursue and shape the course of their own lives, and that respect for diversity of race, gender, religion, and ethnicity is essential to building just societies and vibrant communities.

- That poverty is a consequence of the systemic exclusion of distinct social groups from the rights, resources, and opportunities to achieve their fullest potential.

- That it is our responsibility to foster understanding of the root causes of poverty and injustice and promote the role each individual can play in a global movement for social change.

- That the distinctiveness of our partnerships is defined by mutual respect and a willingness to be innovative, share risks, and assume long-term relationships.

- That it is our obligation to be a responsive, efficient, and effective steward of our donor's resources and apply these resources in a way that will achieve maximum impact.

- That lasting solutions to global problems require sensible management of natural resources to ensure a stable quality of life for generations to come.

- That democratic participation and practice are primary and indispensable elements in enabling people and communities to secure freedom and access to the resources and opportunities they require.

- That it is our responsibility as global citizens to respond to human suffering in all its manifestations and to build an integrated global humanitarian response capability.

On a personal note:

A few years ago a woman working for Childreach (see chapter # 4) came to Illinois to visit with long time donors like us. We used her visit to have a dinner party and invited a table full of interesting people. We had a great evening and have continued supporting Childreach at what we think is a significant level (for us that is supporting five children with monthly contributions).

Well, she has since changed jobs and is currently working with OXFAM. I wrote to her and asked if she would let me know how she likes working with that particular organization.

Here is what she said:

"I truly enjoy working for Oxfam America because my colleagues are so genuinely dedicated to its mission. All international NGOs have a heart, but Oxfam also has a head. Oxfam is seriously committed to the very real but difficult problem of how to create lasting solutions to social problems as large as global poverty and injustice. This struggle requires the best of possible minds—experts in the fields of community resource management, development finance, community organizing, and more. These are the people with whom I am privileged to work. I feel proud of the organization, and through being a part of it, proud of my work.

Oxfam works on the local level empowering grassroots organizations and also at the national, regional and international level. It gives me great satisfaction to see Oxfam's name in the newspapers around the U.S. and Ray Offenheiser, Oxfam America's president, on TV because I know we are having an impact.

The best part of my job is meeting the donors in person who fund Oxfam's important work on behalf of the global poor. This is because I find it spiritually uplifting to meet others who share a charitable and more equitable vision of the world. I never feel like a cog in the wheel at Oxfam like I used to when I worked for the private sector. I know that people overseas, as well as right here in the U.S., will have a better life because of the donation I received today."

Thanks Cyndy!

6.—HEIFER PROJECT INTERNATIONAL
WWW.HEIFER.ORG

Heifer Project International (HPI) has been providing livestock and training to more than four million families around the world for over 50 years. Hpi has more than 300 projects in over 40 countries. They are a non-profit organization that helps people feed themselves, earn income, and care for the environment. Especially around the end-of-year holiday season HPI encourages donations that are identified with particular livestock. A heifer for $500, a Llama for $150, or a trio of rabbits for $60 or a share of any of these and other options give people a choice of what to give.

From the web site:

Heifer International—World Headquarters
P.O. Box 8058, Little Rock, AR/USA 72203
Tel.: 501-907-2600, (800) 422-0474

Heifer International 2000 Annual Report

Heifer animals (and training in their care) offer hungry families around the world a way to feed themselves and become self-reliant. Children receive nutritious milk or eggs; families earn income for school, health care and better housing; communities go beyond meeting immediate needs to fulfilling dreams. Farmers learn sustainable, environmentally sound agricultural techniques.

How Heifer Began
In the 1930s, a civil war raged in Spain. Dan West, a Midwestern farmer and Church of the Brethren youth worker, ladled out cups of milk to hungry children on both sides of the conflict. It struck him that what these families needed was "not a cup, but a cow." He asked his friends back home to donate heifers, a young cow that has not

borne a calf, so hungry families could feed themselves. In return, they could help another family become self-reliant by passing on to them one of their gift animal's female calves.

The idea of giving families a source of food rather than short-term relief caught on and has continued for more than 50 years. As a result, families in 115 countries have enjoyed better health, more income and the joy of helping others.

7.—MICROCREDIT
WWW.MICROCREDITSUMMIT.ORG

Here is an idea whose time has come! Microcredit is making a huge difference in developing countries. The idea is small business loans to assist individuals (or small businesses) in getting started in a commercial venture that can provide a new economic level for the borrower. Often the borrower is a woman who then becomes a significant provider and influence on her neighborhood.

From the web site:

Microcredit is working to ensure that 100 million of the world's poorest families, especially the women of those families, are receiving credit for self-employment and other financial and business services by the year 2005.

Best of the Site

Welcome to Best of the Microcredit Summit Website. This page will direct you to sections of our website that highlight who the Microcredit Summit Campaign is, what the Microcredit Summit Campaign does, and how to get involved.

Get Involved This page tells who we are, what we're about, and how you can join us.

Best Practices This is a section of our newsletter, highlighting leaders from institutions that are demonstrating one or more of the Microcredit Summit's four core themes: reaching the poorest, reaching and empowering women, building financially self-sufficient institutions, and ensuring a positive, measurable impact on the lives of clients and their families. These leaders provide insight into dealing with the challenges that are faced in meeting the core themes.

Institutional Action Plans This is a second section from our newsletter, highlighting the Institutional Action Plan, the basic building block of the Microcredit Summit Campaign. The Institutional Action Plan (IAP) outlines the work an organization has done and intends to do to further the goal and core themes of the Microcredit Summit Campaign. IAPs are submitted annually by members of the Campaign.

Papers Commissioned by the Microcredit Summit These papers were prepared for the Microcredit Summit Campaign by leaders in the field of microcredit. Four of the papers were discussed in plenary sessions on June 24 and June 25, 1999 at the meeting in Abidjan, Côte d'Ivoire, and will be discussed, in updated form, at the Africa, Asia/Pacific, and Latin America regional meetings to be held in 2000 and 2001. The papers highlight and discuss challenges in meeting the core themes of the Summit.

8.—OPPORTUNITY INTERNATIONAL—MICROCREDIT— BATTLING AIDS IN AFRICA

David Simms is chairman of Opportunity International based in Oak Brook, Illinois.

He writes (in an article that was sent to me as part of the LOKOLE newsletter, Oct. 2000—I know not from whence it came) that one potent innovative approach to coping with the AIDS crisis is called "microcredit". Opportunity International is one of the humanitarian agencies that provide microcredit, or small entrepreneurial loans, to the poorest of the working poor in 25 developing countries. As such, they know that a significant cause of the HIV/AIDS infection is poverty, not ignorance. They have learned that economic empowerment, alongside education, can do much to prevent the diseases, particularly AIDS, which emanates from high-risk sexual behavior.

Single women often must rely on transactional sex to meet the economic needs of their families. They engage in high-risk behaviors because immediate family needs outweigh the possible health repercussions.

For example, Kyanja Prossy is raising three of her own children and four AIDS orphans thanks to a dressmaking business; established through a $300 trust bank loan.

The website is: **www.opportunity.org**

From the website for the United States branch of Opportunity International:

Opportunity's Mission, Vision, and Values
Our mission is to provide opportunities for people in chronic poverty to transform their lives. Our strategy is to create jobs, stimulate small business, and strengthen communities among the poor. Our method is

to work through indigenous Partner organizations that provide small business loans, training, and counsel. Our commitment is motivated by Jesus Christ's call to serve the poor. Our core values are respect, commitment to the poor, integrity, and stewardship.

The Evolution of a Dream

Opportunity International seeks transformation in the lives of poor men and women in developing countries. It provides entrepreneurs with access to capital and business training to start and expand small businesses. Opportunity enables people to care for their families and gain the dignity that comes from being self-supporting. Communities are strengthened as local economies improve and entrepreneurs join forces to solve societal problems.

This process is called microenterprise development. The movement was founded and is currently run by entrepreneurs and business people to provide lasting solutions to poverty. In 1971, Al Whittaker, president of Bristol-Myers International Corporation, asked poor people, "What do you need?" They answered, "We need work. With jobs, we will solve our own problems." Whittaker acted on that answer and founded the first Opportunity program in Latin America. In 1976, David Bussau, an Australian entrepreneur, founded a similar job creation program in Indonesia. Three years later, the two programs united. Poor people on two continents proved that with small loans to start up or expand micro-businesses and cottage industries they could support their families.

The Opportunity International Network has now expanded to include 52 Implementing Partners in 25 developing countries and Support Partners in seven developed countries. With a global team in place, the Opportunity Network is capitalizing on the growing popularity of microenterprise development in the public eye. Microenterprise development enables grassroots capitalism. The fundamental premise is that individuals, regardless of their economic status, can improve their income through hard work and free enterprise. Each individual chooses the income-generating activity appropriate to the circumstances. In this way, microenterprise stimulates both individual creativity and personal responsibility.

9.—Save The Children—
WWW.SAVETHECHILDREN.ORG

Several years ago I was the president of the DeKalb County Runners club—an organization of people who liked to run and got together once a month to talk about running and plan some things to do. A couple years in a row we organized a 24 hour relay that was held at the local High School track. We set up tents, we hooked up lights for the middle of the night illumination of at least part of the track, we brought in portapotties and we recruited participants who had teams of people who took turns on the track for 24 hours!

We started Saturday morning and ran until Sunday morning at about 9AM. We had a lot of fun. And we had challenges like an extremely unseasonably cold night when we got heaters from somewhere to help keep the all-nighters warm—those who were running were able to keep warm—it was the lap counters and those waiting in the wings for their running shift to come around on the clock who were cold. Jim and Dan Anderson were a couple of the key runners who set up the site, recruited teams and made the whole event work.

Why am I telling you about these 24 hour relays? The registration fees for the events were donated to support **Save The Children**! I forgot how much money we raised but I still have the pictures in my memory and in some photo albums in the garage!

From the web site:

Our Mission and History

A long history of helping children in need
Across the United States and around the world, **Save the Children** has helped to weave a safety net for an ever-increasing number of children. Beginning at Home

On January 7, 1932 in New York City, Save the Children was created to respond to the needs of the children of coal miners in Appalachia.
Working Abroad
To help European children displaced during World War II, Save the Children provided clothes, milk and food to children and helped communities rebuild in eight European countries.

Native Americans
Save the Children began working with Native Americans in 1948, when a devastating blizzard hit the Navajo Reservation in Arizona.
Technical Assistance
In the late 1950's, Save the Children took a leadership role redefining international development and creating models for the effective transfer of appropriate technology and skills in such areas as sustainable agriculture, small enterprise and health.

High Impact
Save the Children tested a new approach that addressed community-wide needs, such as building roads and improving water supplies, along with needs specific to children in the Dominican Republic in 1972. This "high impact" approach, which facilitated long-term improvements in children's lives, was replicated around the world.

Child Care
Realizing the importance of providing quality child care for children, Save the Children launched the Family Day Care Network in the state of Georgia in 1978. Now serving 7,400 children, the network has trained more than 1,200 low-income family day care providers and helped families identify quality care.

Child Survival
In 1985, Save the Children launched a major child survival initiative to help families to provide better care for their children and to coordinate medical care, water resource development and sanitation improve-

ments. Save the Children's health programs continue to center around child survival, maternal health care and AIDS awareness, as well as nutrition, clean water and sanitation.

Development/Relief

Through the 1980's, Save the Children responded to the needs of children in crisis, as war and natural disasters caused incredible suffering in Asia, Africa and Latin America. Even in the most dire emergency, Save the Children demonstrated that its community development approach could be combined with relief to encourage self-sufficiency and ensure lasting change in the lives of children and their families.

Empowering Women

In the 1990s, Woman/Child Impact was established as the uniting program framework for Save the Children's International Programs. This approach emphasizes that empowering women is key to improving the well-being of children. "Strong Beginnings," a global effort to promote family and community-based early childhood education, was launched.

The Challenge Today

Children today—in the United States and around the world—face greater challenges than ever before. More children are born into poverty and suffer from war and natural disaster than at any other time in modern history. Never has there been such global consensus on the need to protect the rights and well-being of children everywhere.

To help these children get the best possible start in life, Save the Children is promoting locally appropriate programs in education, health care, environmentally sound agriculture, and economic productivity.

10.—UNICEF UNITED NATIONS CHILDREN'S FUND.

"The 6 billionth child born at the turn of the century is likely to have begun a life marked by malnutrition, inadequate of no schooling, poor sanitation, unsafe drinking water, gender discrimination, and abuse. That child is endowed with fundamental human rights. Together we must build a global alliance to ensure those rights—in the knowledge that to serve the best interests of children, we serve the best interests of humanity."—Carol Bellamy, Executive Director, UNICEF.
Unicef has been working for over 50 years on behalf of children. Check out **www.unicef.org** also **www.un.org**

From the UNICEF web site on October 16, 2001:

Afghan Region: UNICEF Ready to Assist

Along with the rest of the United Nations family, UNICEF is ready to provide humanitarian relief in the Afghanistan region as soon as the situation allows. UNICEF field offices throughout the region have been pre-positioning relief supplies and preparing to assist children and women both inside Afghanistan and in neighboring countries, as needed.
One of those offices, a field unit in the town of Quetta, Pakistan, was burned by a mob during street demonstrations on Monday 8 October. No UNICEF staff were in the office at the time and no one was injured. An adjacent office of the UN refugee agency (UNHCR) was stoned during the incident.
As the situation stabilizes and as more information about humanitarian needs becomes available, UNICEF and its sister agencies will work to deliver food, medicine, clothing, blankets, water purification tablets and other vital relief.

Read more about UNICEF's ongoing humanitarian relief activities in the Afghanistan region in **UNICEF's Afghan pages.** (**http://www.unicef.org/noteworthy/afghanistan/**)

11.—CARE

The name of this organization has become a household word. When we send a package of goodies to our child at school, to a relative, to someone far away, we often refer to it as a "care" package. The name comes form this organization—**www.care.org**

From the web site:

About CARE:
CARE is one of the world's largest private international relief and development organizations. Founded in the aftermath of World War II, CARE enabled Americans to send more than 100 million CARE Packages® to survivors of the conflict in Europe and Asia. CARE has become a leader in sustainable development and emergency aid, reaching tens of millions of people each year in more than 60 countries in Africa, Asia, Europe and Latin America. For more than 50 years now, CARE has been a vehicle of American generosity abroad.

CARE reaches out to people whose lives are devastated by humanitarian emergencies, or who are struggling each day in poor communities to survive and improve their lives. CARE focuses its approach at the family and community levels. We believe that each family should enjoy a basic level of livelihood security. This means that every family should have:

- Food;

- Health care;

- A place to live;

- Education;

- A safe and healthy environment; and,

- The ability to participate in decisions affecting their family, community and country.

CARE's programs seek to help poor families obtain this security. CARE seeks a world of tolerance and social justice, where people have overcome poverty and live in dignity and security.

Why Support CARE?

The Faces of CARE: Each year, around the world, CARE provides hope and opportunity to tens of millions of men, women and children.

Lasting Results: CARE's programs are based on partnerships emphasizing community participation and capacity-building, both factors that have proven critical to local ownership and sustainability. CARE programs leave a lasting legacy in human and social capital.

Excellence in Action: CARE looks at the big picture of poverty and combines approaches to attack not just the symptoms, but the underlying causes as well. This holistic approach results in diverse and innovative solutions, including programs that build capacities of local organizations, which advance girls' education and equity for women, that promote land mine safety and conflict resolution and that integrate human rights concerns with humanitarian assistance.

Global Reach: CARE is one of the largest private international relief and development organizations in the world. Together with our partners from CARE International and hundreds of local organizations, we have the skills and organizational reach to make a significant impact on poverty.

Efficiency and Accountability: More than 90 percent of CARE's expended resources support program activities. Less than 10 percent of expended resources support administrative and fundraising expenditures. We conform to the highest accounting and financial standards.

Credibility and Experience: CARE has more than 50 years of experience working with poor families and communities. Every U.S. president since Harry Truman has endorsed our work. The United Nations, the European Community and other international organizations often turn to CARE to implement programs.

Flexibility: CARE's long and wide-ranging experience means that we can respond quickly and effectively to a full range of situations, from providing lifesaving emergency relief, to rehabilitation in the wake of disaster, to support for long-term development.

Independence: CARE is a private, nonprofit organization. We are not affiliated with any government agency, religious group or other entity. Our overriding goal is to help poor families improve their lives.

Advocacy: CARE has the international stature and public support to help influence policy decisions in the United States and overseas. Our on-the-ground experience and independence lend us nonpartisan credibility and respect. We use these, very selectively, to advocate in favor of policies that will help foster development, peace and justice.

Our Promise
Your support of CARE is a critical catalyst to worldwide programs that provide relief and alleviate poverty. In carrying out this work, we are committed to upholding the highest standards of respect, integrity, commitment and excellence.
Click here to view CARE's Privacy Policy.
Click here for CARE's Terms and Conditions.

CARE
151 Ellis Street NE
Atlanta, GA 30303-2439
1-800-521-CARE, ext. 999
info@care.org

12.—FOUNDATION FOR INTERNATIONAL COMMUNITY ASSISTANCE— WWW.VILLAGEBANKING.ORG

Stories about how a small loan has made a successful businesswoman or man out of an African villager bring a smile to my heart. How wonderful to be able to make such a big difference in someone's life with such a small amount of seed money. These loans are a way to move the world using powerful leverage. These loans enable people to achieve economic freedom beyond the end of hunger!

From the web site:

FINCA Mission: **FINCA** (The Foundation for International Community Assistance) has been helping families to create their own solutions to poverty since 1984. FINCA is: **An anti-poverty organization.** Our work is aimed at creating employment, raising family incomes, and reducing poverty worldwide. **A provider of financial services to low-income families.** We offer small loans and a savings program to those turned down by traditional banks, believing that even the poor have a right to financial services. With these loans, families can invest in, and build, their own small businesses and their income-earning capacity. Worldwide, our clients post repayment rates over 96%. **A leader.** FINCA invented the "Village Banking™ method" of credit delivery, now used by more than 80 other organizations worldwide. We operate on five continents in more diverse cultures than any other microcredit provider. *Not* **a typical charity.** We offer loans, not gifts, and we promote financial independence, both among our clients and in our programs. Although we are a nonprofit, we strive to operate using sound business principles and an entrepreneurial spirit. Our mission: FINCA provides financial services to the world's poorest families so they can create their own jobs, raise household incomes, and improve their standard of living. We deliver these services through a global network of

locally managed, self-supporting institutions. Our work:
Enables poor families to create their own solutions to poverty.
Provides small solutions-loans of $50-$1,000-**and multiplies them a million times. Promotes community and individual development**: FINCA Village Banking groups-borrowing groups of 10-50 neighbors-promote the success of entire communities. **Requires a partnership** between a family who wants to escape poverty, and another family willing to finance the small loan that gives them that opportunity.

13.—Appropriate Technology— WWW.APPROTEC.ORG

Martin Fisher with Nick Moon co-founded a company that produces appropriate technology for the Kenyan economy. At least that is the focus of an article in the November/December 2000 issue of *The Stanford Magazine* (p. 44). The company, ApproTEC, makes foot operated pumps for small farmers in Kenya to use for irrigating their fields. The pumps work and are affordable. Check the web site for the most up to date information and for ways to get involved. **www.approtec.org**

From the web site:

Under **what's new** on the web site—Martin Fisher and Nick Moon, ApproTEC's founders, have been selected as **Schwab Outstanding Social Entrepreneurs for 2003.** Martin and Nick will attend the World Economic Forum in Davos, Switzerland in January, 2003 as guests of the Schwab Foundation.

ApproTEC's mission is to promote sustainable economic growth and employment creation in Kenya and other countries by developing and promoting technologies which can be used by dynamic entrepreneurs to establish and run profitable small scale enterprises.

ApproTEC believes that self-motivated private entrepreneurs managing small-scale enterprises are the most effective agents for developing emergent economies.

These entrepreneurs can raise small amounts of capital ($100-$1,000 US) to start a new small enterprise and can manage the day-to-day affairs of such a business. However, it is difficult for them to identify viable business opportunities, to access the technologies required to launch the new enterprises and to widely market new products. Appro-TEC helps them in these vital areas.

In addition to promoting small enterprise development, ApproTEC's technologies, expertise and methods are widely applied throughout Africa to support programs in agriculture, shelter, water, sanitation, health and relief.

The Organization

ApproTEC is a development Non-Governmental/Non-Profit Organization (NGO) which was founded in Kenya in July 1991. Presently ApproTEC has over 50 employees including market researchers, engineers, trainers, promoters and administrative staff. We have our head office and a workshop in Nairobi, Kenya and project offices in Western and Central Kenya. New offices are planned for Arusha, Tanzania and Kampala, Uganda.

ApproTEC over the years has developed expertise in various sectors. Technologies and enterprise opportunities developed and promoted by ApproTEC include:

- **Oil Processing Technologies:** ApproTEC's manually operated Mafuta Mali (translates from Swahili as "oil wealth") oilseed press has proved to be the most popular processor of cooking oil from locally grown oilseeds such as sunflower and sesame (simsim) in the East and Central African region. To date (April 2000) over 905 such presses have been sold.

- **Micro-Irrigation Technologies:** Since 1996 ApproTEC has been the leader in micro-irrigation technologies through the development and sales of its popularly known series of MoneyMaker pumps. To date (2003) over 27,000 such pumps have been sold. ApproTEC is developing more of these micro-irrigation technologies.

- **Building Technologies:** ApproTEC-developed technologies for low cost construction, such as the Stabilized Soil Blocks technology, continue to dominate in the region. Over 1,000 manual block-making ActionPack Block presses have been sold throughout Rwanda, Burundi and Malawi. In Malawi, the technology has been adopted for school construction in selected projects. Other construction technologies in which ApproTEC has expertise include Rammed Earth, Burnt Bricks, Micro Concrete Roofing and Hollow Concrete Blocks.

- **Water & Sanitation Technologies:** ApproTEC expertise in this area includes Domed Pit Latrine Slabs for sanitation and construction of ferro-cement Water tanks.

- **Other Technologies:** ApproTEC is continuing to develop new technologies such as a manual hay-baler, a deep-well pump, and avocado cosmetics.

ApproTEC staff continually search for new opportunities and develop new technologies and business packages. For technologies that are already developed, ApproTEC hopes to raise funds to promote the commercialisation and further dissemination of these technologies, in order to create more new enterprises and jobs in the region.

14.—THE SOCIETY FOR INTERNATIONAL DEVELOPMENT
WWW.SIDINT.ORG

My wife and I just received an email from friends:
Dear ones,
In the interest of expanding the global community here in the Chicago area, please consider joining this group. Membership is $20 annually, meetings are the second Tuesday of the month, and programs are fascinating. If for no other reason than educating ourselves in the areas of our impossible promises, it appears to be well worth the investment in time. Neil and I have just joined.

ISID works to promote awareness of international development issues in Illinois and to encourage networking and discussion.

What do YOU want in terms of international development in Chicago? "Chicago" and "International Development" do not seem to go together. But they do. The Illinois Society for International Development (ISID), along with other committed organizations, is changing the way we mobilize to address development issues overseas.

Recent programs have focused on International Health, Refugee Resettlement in Chicago, Advocacy, Chicago's Response to the Crisis in the Horn of Africa, Global Dimensions of Environmental Restoration, many others.
Web site, **www.sidint.org**, has the following overview:

From the web site:

Overview
Created in 1957, the Society for International Development (SID) is a unique global network of individuals and institutions concerned with development which is participatory, pluralistic and sustainable. SID

has over 3,000 individual members in 125 countries, 55 institutional members and 65 local chapters. It works with more than 100 associations, networks and institutions involving academia, parliamentarians, students, political leaders and development experts, both at local and international levels. This makes SID one of the very few organizations that has a holistic, multidisciplinary and multi-sectorial approach to development and social change.

SID's purpose is to:

- To support development innovation at all levels—local, national, global—in order to contribute to the search for solutions to the problems of poverty, injustice gender inequity and lack of sustainability;

- To encourage, support and facilitate the creation of a sense of community amongst individuals and organizations committed to social justice at the local, national, regional and international levels;

- To promote the sharing of knowledge, dialogue, understanding and co-operation for social and economic development that furthers the well-being of all peoples.

In pursuing this purpose, SID sees its role as:

- A bridge between diverse constituencies in the search for social justice: (including grassroots movements, academia, policy-makers, progressive business sector, multilateral institutions), as well as between the local and the global;

- A global catalyst for civil society: SID aims to mobilize and strengthen civil society groups by actively building partnerships among them and with other sectors;

- A knowledge broker: SID supports the generation of knowledge on innovative development initiatives, concepts and practices, and stimulates exchanges and dissemination at all levels and across sectors.

15.—St. John of God Missions—in 46 Countries Around the World
WWW.STJOHNOFGOD.ORG.

From the brochure:

The St. John of God Missions—For over 500 years the Brothers of the Hospitaller Order of St. Johns of God have been reaching out to touch the lives of those in need. As an integral part of the St. John of God Missions, the Brothers provide care for tens of thousands of people across the globe that are sick, mentally ill, have physical or mental disabilities, and are homeless or poor.

The presence of St. John of God Missions is felt in over 250 hospitals and centres in 49 countries around the world, where the Brothers exemplify the works of St. John of God—striving to create an environment of caring and hospitality, while empowering others to help themselves.

John Ciudad was born in 1495, and after a life as a drifter, shepherd, soldier, and bookseller, experienced a religious conversion so dramatic that his behavior appeared bizarre to others, and forced him to be placed in a mental institution. His stay there gave witness to the cruel and inhumane treatment those with mental disorders suffered and he vowed to help those suffering on his release. Now known as St. John of God, his commitment to treat the disabled, sick, mentally ill and disadvantaged *with dignity and compassion* is the cornerstone upon which the St. John of God Missions is built.

St. John of God Missions
Hospitaller Brothers of St. John of God
P.O. Box 2001
Deptford, NJ 08096 1-800-532-4483

And from the web site:

Mission

Springing from the Christian values and holistic approach advocated and practiced by its founders, the Hospitaller Order of St. John of God is dedicated to the provision of health, social, education, and welfare services. It has a mission to ensure that persons availing of its services receive the highest quality care, education, training, treatment or assistance in accordance with their needs.

Philosophy

The philosophy of the Order's services is that people are the creation of God, with intrinsic value and inherent dignity. This philosophy is based on the beliefs and values of the Order's founder, St. John of God.

Section III
Support Efforts Focused on
Particular Important Issues

16.—FIGHT HATE AND PROMOTE TOLERANCE— WWW.TOLERANCE.ORG

This web site includes 101 Tools For Tolerance. Sound familiar? I guess it makes sense that one of the "101" ways to participate in making the world work would be "101" tools for tolerance.

Now, tolerance is one level of accepting each other's differences. So I suppose it is OK to start there. But, how about celebrating each other and our differences? Wouldn't that be great and a step beyond tolerance?

From the web site:

Check out 101 ways to help foster tolerance in yourself, your family, your schools, your workplace and your community. Then tell us what works for you and your community. Go

> **/tol watch/index.jsp/tol watch/index.jsp**
>
>> **Hate in the news**
>>
>> **Tolerance in the news**
>>
>> **Track hate across America**
>>
>> **Learn the truth about hate sites**
>
> **/do something/index.html/do something/index.html**
>
>> **10 Ways to Fight Hate**
>>
>> **Find a human rights group**
>>
>> **101 Tools for Tolerance**
>>
>> **Speak up—Join our Forums**
>
> **/dig deeper/index.html/dig deeper/index.html**

<u>Explore your hidden biases</u>

<u>Explore hidden history</u>

<u>Teach tolerance at home</u>

<u>Remember the Civil Rights Movement</u>

17.—SIMON WIESENTHAL CENTER—COMBATING HATE— WWW.WIESENTHAL.COM

Where does hate come from? I can not imagine we are born with it. It has to come from what we are taught either directly or indirectly. Either we see/hear/feel our parents hating or it shows up in our cultural environment. Somehow we acquire hate and now we know it only gets in the way of a world that works. Whatever can be done to combat (and eliminate) hate—must be done! (see #106)

From the web site:

The Simon Wiesenthal Center is an international Jewish human rights organization dedicated to preserving the memory of the Holocaust by fostering tolerance and understanding through community involvement, educational outreach and social action. The Center confronts important contemporary issues including racism, anti-Semitism, terrorism and genocide and is accredited as an NGO both at the United Nations and UNESCO. With a membership of over 400,000 families, the Center is headquartered in Los Angeles and maintains offices in New York, Toronto, Miami, Jerusalem, Paris and Buenos Aires.

Established in 1977, the Center closely interacts on an ongoing basis with a variety of public and private agencies, meeting with elected officials, the U.S. and foreign governments, diplomats and heads of state. Other issues that the Center deals with include: the prosecution of Nazi war criminals; Holocaust and tolerance education; Middle East Affairs; and extremist groups, neo-Nazism, and hate on the Internet.

The International headquarters are based in Los Angeles, California.
1399 South Roxbury Drive
Los Angeles, California 90035
310 553.9036

800 900.9036 (toll-free from within the U.S.)
310 553.4521 (fax)
information@wiesenthal.net

18.—THE GLOBAL HEALTH ALLIANCE—WWW.GLBHEALTH.ORG

The ad for "Global Health Alliance" that I saw in a magazine had a picture of a woman on a horse with this caption: "The sweetest words Kathy Dickerson's ever heard? 'We don't need you anymore.'" That (to not be needed any more) should be the goal of all the organizations formed to resolve the problems of hunger, malnutrition, poverty, and all these issues that are being addressed by the organizations in this book.

From the web site:

Global Health Alliance IMPROVING HUMAN AND ENVIRONMENTAL HEALTH

There is a profound cycle of poverty, poor health, and diminishing natural resources in developing countries. Global Health Alliance (GHA) is dedicated to breaking this cycle by improving both human and environmental health. *Renewable energy is the common denominator!* **ON-LINE REVIEWS** are listed under Agency for Environmental Health, now doing business as Global Health Alliance. GUIDESTAR FOUNDATION CENTER **Our Mission: Improve human and environmental health** in developing countries through community-based education programs and activities that demonstrate the relationship between the two. GHA was formed in 1998, in direct response to requests of rural Nicaraguan communities. Mothers sought ways to improve health services for their children while men requested technical assistance in improving their crop yields. Simple requests you ask? Absolutely. Which is why we are able to achieve great results on an annual budget of roughly $20,000. **GHA operates with a purely volunteer staff, allowing for the greatest amount of resources to be used for local projects.** While providing education about alternative methods, GHA also supports communities in their development. The women wanted better health services for their children, but there was no electricity in the community. **Given the choice between expensive projects that they could not afford to maintain or utilizing existing resources, harnessing the sun became the obvious choice.** Our adopted methodology involves the community in the projects, and gives them a voice in the direction of the project as well. GHA purchases all project materials locally, supporting the local economy and ensuring the availability of materials. Local renewable energy technicians are used exclusively.

19.—SUPPORT A MISSION PROGRAM
THROUGH A CHURCH E.G.
WWW.GLOBALMINISTRIES.ORG

One example of a mission program is the Christian Church (Division of Overseas Ministries) that supports work in Africa as well as other continents. Recently I received a letter from Patricia Tucker, President of the Division of Overseas Ministries with offices in Indianapolis (email: dom@disciples.org). The letter included a report from a woman working in South Africa with the Centre for Constructive Theology of the University of Durban-Westville. She told of her experience on a hot summer day in Hlotse when she attended a church service in Sesotho and watched as the congregation gave and gave to contribute to the work of the church. Patricia went on to say: "There are many uplifting ministries taking place around the world, thanks in part to the exchange of talents and gifts between the Division of Overseas Ministries and International partners." In particular I noticed the reference to the **exchange with International Partners**. I believe the cooperation and exchange between all the organizations working to improve the lot of others around the world will accomplish more than the individual efforts through the synergy that is happening naturally.

Of course my personal bias is towards mission work that works with the indigenous populations to raise their standard of living in ways appropriate to their culture and country's resources.

That is the sort of work that my parents did in the Congo from about 1929 to 1963. In fact, the Division of Overseas Ministries mentioned above was the organization that they worked through. Our address was:

> Lotumbe, DCCM
> Coquilhatville
> Congo Belge, Africa

Lotumbe was the village we lived in and Coquilhatville was the regional capital city downriver about two days by sternwheeler. Three or four days going up-river.

The DCCM stood for The Disciples of Christ Congo Mission. I believe the value brought to mission work like my parents did was the education and support for improved sanitation, agriculture, health care, and life support systems. The spiritual support, the new (to the Congolese) look at religion was the vehicle on which all the other benefits of their work were carried.

20.—AMNESTY INTERNATIONAL
WWW.AIUSA.ORG
AMNESTY INTERNATIONAL—
WWW.AMNESTYUSA.ORG

I remember hearing a radio ad (no doubt on NPR) for Amnesty International several years ago. They were telling a little about what the organization does and asking for donations. What I remember the most is that they asked us, whether we donate or not, to make a toast the next time we are out with our friends. A toast "To Freedom"!

My wife and I now do this frequently, propose a toast "to freedom". It helps us remember the freedoms we enjoy as citizens of the USA that most people in the world do not enjoy to the same extent. So, "To Freedom!"

Founded in London in 1961, Amnesty International is a Nobel Prize-winning grassroots activist organization with over one million members worldwide. Amnesty International is dedicated to freeing prisoners of conscience, gaining fair trials for political prisoners, ending torture, political killings and "disappearances," and abolishing the death penalty throughout the world. Amnesty International USA (AIUSA) is the U.S. Section of Amnesty International.

From the web site:

Amnesty's Roots
By Linda Rabben

AIUSA activist Linda Rabben has written a book, *Fierce Legion of Friends: A History of Human Rights Campaigns and Campaigners,* which will be published this year by the Quixote Center to commemorate Amnesty's 40th anniversary.

According to Amnesty International's "creation myth," one day in late 1960, a British lawyer named Peter Benenson was reading the Daily Telegraph in the London tube, when he saw a brief article about two Portuguese students who had been arrested for making a toast to freedom in a Lisbon bar. He decided to start an organization to rescue political prisoners and other victims of government repression around the world.

In May 1961, Benenson published an article, "The Forgotten Prisoners," in the London *Observer*. According to the myth, thousands of people responded, and Benenson set up Amnesty. Soon its members were writing so many letters to heads of state and other officials that political prisoners were being released all over the world. A member designed the organization's logo, a candle circled by barbed wire. AI became the world's most successful, largest and most influential human rights organization, winning the Nobel Peace Prize in 1977. Amnesty's members commemorate the circumstances of its founding by ending every Annual General Meeting with a "toast to freedom." The creation myth does have a large kernel of truth, but the real story of Amnesty's beginnings is much more complex. Its distinctive goals and strategies owe much to earlier campaigns and organizations. Whether unconsciously or deliberately, Benenson and his friends were responding or reacting to earlier successes and failures by recreating old structures or inventing new ones.

21.—HABITAT FOR HUMANITY
WWW.HABITATFORHUMANITY.ORG

Habitat for Humanity is a world-wide organization that is know best for assisting families get into their own new home with sweat equity in the home and pride of ownership that is otherwise very difficult for those that work with the organization. There are many local organizations. For example, in the county where I live there is the DuPage Habitat for Humanity.

Their Vision Statement is:

"To make Dupage County a better place to live by building Community."

Their Mission Statement:

"The mission of DuPage Habitat for Humanity is to provide home ownership opportunities to limited income families or individuals and to put the reality of substandard housing in the minds and hearts of DuPage residents in such a powerful way that unattainable home ownership for these individuals becomes politically, socially and religiously unacceptable."

Ex-President Jimmy Carter has been very active with Habitat through the Carter Center.

Check out the web site **www.habitatforhumanity.org**!!

From the web site:

Habitat for Humanity International is a nonprofit, nondenominational Christian housing organization.

We welcome all people to join us as we build simple, decent, affordable, houses in partnership with those in need of adequate shelter.

Since 1976, Habitat has built more than 100,000 houses in more than 60 countries, including some 30,000 houses across the United States.

This year, 2001, the new president has also demonstrated support for Habitat for Humanity. George (Dubya) Bush spent a part of a day on a job site for Habitat and pounded a few nails **and** his thumb for the cause.

22.—THE EDUCATION NETWORK (412)242-9555 WWW.THEEDUCATIONNETWORK.ORG

According to documentation from The Education Network:
The purpose of the Education Network is to give people the power to create environments, which allow for the success of all learners. We have concentrated on defining and utilizing a rigorous framework of thinking, speaking and listening that enables people to create a new future for education. We employ this technology to:

• provide opportunities for individuals and communities to invent their accountability for education;

• support all stakeholders in education in producing results consistent with their vision;

• empower educators to produce extraordinary results in the classroom;

• foster participation in education by entire communities: and,

• Promote collaboration and communication among individuals, organizations and communities engaged in the transformation of education.

To fulfill their purpose, the education network implements their technology in two key ways. First, they train volunteers to play strategic, catalytic roles in their communities. The volunteers provide leadership that inspires possibilities, nurtures the commitments of others, and stimulates creativity and achievement. Two, they deliver programs designed to break up old patterns of action, foster new ways of thinking and empower people to achieve concrete breakthroughs. The following programs address diverse commitments and produce reliable results.

- Access to Breakthrough Teaching...

- The Future by Design...

- Leadership for Education...

To find out more about "The Education Network" contact Robin Carson, Executive Director, at
7033 Meade Place #8
Pittsburgh, PA 15208
(412) 242-9555

As of October 3rd, 2001, the website says the following:

> Welcome to the new ***www.theeducationnetwork.org*** website! Our site has been recently created and will soon be available for your use. Our web designers are creating a new web-interface that will soon be online! In the meantime, please be patient while we are working to make these changes. A new page will be available soon!

As of April 30, 2002 the website is up and running and it looks great!

23.—International Rescue Committee
www.theIRC.org

"You have 30 minutes to pack everything you own. If you and your family can't carry it on your backs, it will have to stay behind.
Look around one last time because you may never return to this home again.
And, be careful what route you take. Choose wrong and you and your family could perish by nightfall…"
This quote is from a recent letter from the IRC that described a recent experience in Kosovo. Such experiences are not unique to that region either.
I recall that in 1960 my parents who were back in the Belgian Congo (in 1960 the country was given its freedom from Belgian rule) as it became an independent country. The United States Embassy provided for all US citizens to be evacuated in 1960 as with freedom and independence came much turmoil and bloodshed.
My mother and father had overnight rather than the 30 minutes mentioned above but it was the same experience. They never got to go back to their home. Each could take one suitcase.

The IRC is currently assisting uprooted people in over 30 countries around the world.

A recent fundraising letter says they have reduced their administrative and fundraising costs to the point that 92% of every dollar donated goes straight to their programs.

IRC, 122 East 42nd Street, New York, NY 10168-1289

I recently contacted the IRC and received this response—Thanks Alisha.

"Dear Mr. Smith:

Thank you for your interest in the IRC and considering the organization for you book.

I'm sending out to you today a copy of our current annual report and two recent articles, from Money and Smart Money magazines, on the IRC's efficiency.

In addition to supporting the IRC financially, one can volunteer with any of our domestic refugee resettlement offices or occasionally with programs overseas. More information on volunteering can be found on our web site <**www.theIRC.org**>.

As to why the IRC should be included in your book, I've listed below a few quotations from some of the IRC's most prominent supporters:

"Freedom has no better friend than the International Rescue Committee."

—(Then) U.S. Secretary of State Madeleine Albright

New York, November 10, 1998

"Right from the beginning, I was struck by the personal attention and extraordinary decency with which they treated me, a lonely immigrant youth in Vienna, a city overrun with hundreds of thousands of refugees....As wars, revolutions and civil wars sweep the globe, the International Rescue Committee and its volunteers seem to be at their sites doing their work. Every time I read about a new wave of refugees, Vietnamese, Chinese, Russian Jews, Croatians, it brings to mind my experience with them. Generations of IRC volunteers and workers are ceaselessly doing for others what they did for me."

-Andrew Grove, Chairman of Intel, who was assisted by the IRC in Vienna in December 1956 and resettled in the U.S. by the IRC in January 1957. He has supported the IRC financially since 1964 and has been a board member since 1999.

"What makes the IRC special in my mind is that once it begins to help refugees in a certain area of the world, it will not leave until is sure it is no
longer needed. IRC does not chase headlines. It goes to-and stays in-places
no one wants to be."
—Colin L. Powell
October 28, 1996

Please let us know when your book comes out. If you have any further
questions, or need additional information, I can be reached at Tel: 212-551-
0969, email <alisha@theIRC.org>.

Best regards,
Alisha Lumea
Public Education Specialist
International Rescue Committee
122 East 42nd Street
New York, NY 10168
Tel: 212-551-0969
alisha@theIRC.org
www.theIRC.org

24.—INVESTING IN PEOPLE—INVESTING IN THE FUTURE—THE ECONOMIC COMMISSION FOR AFRICA WWW.UN.ORG/DEPTS/ECA

This was the title of an address by K. Y. Amoako, Executive Secretary of the Economic Commission for Africa (the ECA), to the 72nd Ordinary Session of the Council of Ministers of the Organization of African Unity, on the 6th of July, 2000 in Tome, Togo, Africa.

In his talk he points out the ECA's analysis shows that low levels of investment in education and health have been identified as major impediments to growth and development and are "at the core" of the initial conditions that must be addressed.

- Average per capita spending on education in Africa declined from $41 in 1980 to $25 in 1995 in real terms.

- Some of the goals that have been set (and that need renewed commitment since we are far from achieving them):

- Halving poverty by 2015, a centerpiece of the social summit process: Presently, forty percent of Africans live below the poverty line. The majority are women. Economies need to grow at 8% per year to achieve this goal.

- Eradicating, eliminating or controlling major diseases constituting global health problems by 2000: AIDS is increasing at an alarming rate in Africa, especially among women. Malaria, which elsewhere in the world is on the decline, is increasing its deadly reach in Africa.

- Providing universal primary education by 2015: Enrollment rates for Sub Saharan Africa stand at 73 percent.

- Eliminating gender disparities in secondary education by 2005: According to UNIFEM'S "Progress of the World's Women" only

five out of 34 countries for which data could be found have suc-
ceeded in doing this. In ten of these countries, there had been a
decline in female enrollment rates over the last decade.

The following web site is a pointer to several documents by K. Y. Amo-
aka.

**http://www.uneca.org/eca_resources/Publications/books/
perspectives_on_africa_s_development/default.htm**

25.—THE BUREAU OF ECONOMIC AND BUSINESS AFFAIRS
HTTP://WWW.STATE.GOV/E/EB/

The Bureau of Economic and Business Affairs is in the US State Department.

From the web site:

The Bureau of Economic and Business Affairs (EB) formulates and carries out U.S. foreign economic policy, integrating U.S. economic interests with our foreign policy goals so that U.S. firms and investors can compete on an equal basis with their counterparts overseas. It implements American economic policy in cooperation with U.S. companies, U.S. Government agencies, and other organizations. Under the direction of Assistant Secretary **E. Anthony Wayne**, the bureau negotiates agreements with foreign governments and advances U.S. positions in such international organizations as the International Monetary Fund or World Trade Organization. EB officers:

- Work with the World Trade Organization to establish fair rules of international trade

- Lead U.S. negotiations on bilateral civil aviation treaties

- Negotiate bilateral and regional investment treaties in partnership with USTR

- Combat bribery in international commerce; and

- Coordinate issues related to economic sanctions.

The EB Bureau's organizational structure consists of five units, each headed by a Deputy Assistant Secretary:

- Energy, Sanctions and Commodities (EB/ESC);

- International Communications and Information Policy (EB/CIP);

- International Finance and Development (EB/IFD);

- Trade Policy and Programs (EB/TPP);

- Transportation Affairs (EB/TRA).

Civil and Foreign Service officers and support staff bring a wide variety of educational and private sector backgrounds to offices in Washington, DC. They develop U.S. policy, administer programs, negotiate, and represent the Department before Congress, U.S. business and industry, and international organizations. Overseas, embassy economic officers lay the groundwork for negotiations, report on economic trends and the commercial climate, and maintain constant contact with foreign governments to represent U.S. interests.

26.—THE STATE OF THE WORLDS CHILDREN
WWW.UNICEF.ORG/SOWC00

Statistical tables are available on-line at the web site.

From the web site:

The State of the World's Children 2000 seeks to fan the flame that burned so brilliantly a decade ago when world leaders adopted the Convention on the Rights of the Child in 1989 and then confirmed their commitments for children and adolescents at the 1990 World Summit for Children. It is a call to leaders in industrialized and developing countries alike to reaffirm their promises for children. It is a call for vision and leadership within families and communities, where the respect for the rights of children and women is first born and nurtured and where the protection of those rights begins. And it is a call to all people to realize a new dream within a single generation: a shared vision of children and women—indeed of humankind—freed from poverty and discrimination, freed from violence and disease.
And in 2001 an updated web site at **www.unicef.org/sowc01**
And in 2002 an updated web site at **www.unicef.org/sowc02**
From that web site:

Early childhood

What happens during the very earliest years of a child's life, from birth to age 3, influences how the rest of childhood and adolescence unfolds. Yet, this critical time is usually neglected in the policies, programmes and budgets of countries.

Drawing on reports from the world over, *The State of the World's Children 2001* details the daily lives of parents and other caregivers who are striving—in the face of war, poverty and the HIV/AIDS epidemic—to protect the rights and meet the needs of these young children.

27.—HUMAN RIGHTS WATCH
WWW.HRW.ORG

See if there is something for you to do with or in support of this organization:

From the web site:

Human Rights Watch is dedicated to protecting the human rights of people around the world.
We stand with victims and activists to prevent discrimination, to uphold political freedom, to protect people from inhumane conduct in wartime, and to bring offenders to justice.
We investigate and expose human rights violations and hold abusers accountable.
We challenge governments and those who hold power to end abusive practices and respect international human rights law.
We enlist the public and the international community to support the cause of human rights for all.

(New York, September 16, 2002) United Nations General Assembly member states should emphasize political reform and respect for human rights over traditional economic development initiatives, Human Rights Watch said today.

28—THE SOUTHERN POVERTY LAW CENTER
WWW.SPLCENTER.ORG

This organization can use your donations and your participation to further its causes—including "Teaching Tolerance".

From the web site:

The Southern Poverty Law Center is a nonprofit organization that combats hate, intolerance and discrimination through education and litigation. Its programs include the Intelligence Project, Teaching Tolerance and Tolerance.org. The Center also sponsors the Civil Rights Memorial, which celebrates the memory of those who died during the Civil Rights Movement.

In response to an alarming increase in hate crime among youth, the Southern Poverty Law Center began the Teaching Tolerance project in 1991 as an extension of the Center's legal and educational efforts. Through the generous support of Center donors, Teaching Tolerance offers free or low-cost resources to educators at all levels. *Teaching Tolerance* magazine is distributed free twice a year to more than a half-million educators throughout the U.S. and in 70 other countries. Its editors welcome contributions of writing and artwork that address classroom themes of tolerance, respect and community building. Curriculum resources include the free video-and-text teaching kits *America's Civil Rights Movement* and *The Shadow of Hate,* which chronicle the history of hatred and intolerance in America and the struggle to overcome prejudice. A third teaching kit, *Starting Small,* is a teacher-training package for early childhood educators. Other Teaching Tolerance resources include a free set of eight full-color *One World* posters with teacher's guide and the 64-page *Responding to Hate at School*: A Guide for Teachers, Counselors and Administrators. The project offers grants of up to $2.000 for K-12 teachers and a one-year research fel-

<u>lowship</u> for educators with strong writing skills and an interest in equity issues.

29.—United Nations High Commissioner for Refugees— WWW.USAFORUNHCR.ORG

This is another organization to which one can donate funds that will assist those in dire need. This organization gets most of its budget from voluntary donations by donor governments, and they also need private donations to keep up with the demand for assistance to refugees. The mailing I received was all about the need to assist refugees in Chechnya. Additional needs happen all over—until we get this planet to work!

From the web site:

What We Do

Established by concerned American citizens, USA for UNHCR builds support in the United States for the humanitarian work of UNHCR and its partners. Our mission is to raise the consciousness of Americans about the **work and accomplishments** of the United Nations High Commissioner for Refugees (UNHCR) through education and advocacy. We want to give individual Americans, frustrated by the growing refugee crisis and their own inability to do something to help, a way to put action behind their words. See the **Action Page**!

UNHCR is responsible for protecting over 22 million people worldwide, including refugees, internally displaced people and former refugees who are returning to their homes. As the largest international humanitarian organization, UNHCR and its 400+partners provide food, water, shelter, medical and other types of assistance to refugees worldwide. UNHCR operates in 122 countries. When governments are unable or unwilling to protect their own citizens, UNHCR helps refugees find safety and the means to begin a normal life again.

UNHCR proactively establishes an international presence in countries on the verge of serious conflict in order to confront problems before populations have been uprooted. Other than actual prevention of refugee crises, the optimal solution for refugees is to be able to return to their home countries, voluntarily and in safety and dignity. In many cases, UNHCR helps refugees to survive in countries of first asylum until the political situation in their home country is resolved and they can safely return home. UNHCR and its partner organizations do not leave refugees at the border but actively help them reintegrate back into their countries of origin. The next best option is for refugees to remain in a country of first asylum, successfully integrate into their new environment and rebuild their lives there. For a small number of refugees, however, the only way to ensure their safety and a viable future is through resettlement to third countries.

30.—SPECIAL OLYMPICS
WWW.SPECIALOLYMPICS.ORG

Most of us, I'm sure, have heard of the Special Olympics. One of the recent stories (possibly apocryphal) that had been being passed around via email is about the child who was in a group of nine Special Olympics contestants in a 100 yard dash. This young lad tripped and fell after about 15 or 20 yards of heroic effort. As he lay on the track in tears at his failure, the other eight children heard his wails and turned to see what happened. They all, all eight of them, turned, ran back to their fallen comrade and helped him up. Then they all nine, with linked arms, ran all the way to the finish line together. Who won that race? Friends of mine have assisted at Special Olympics events and have reported being inspired and moved in ways not often felt. This is an organization that makes the planet work for those of us who do not have all the physical and mental gifts that others have.

From the web site: © Special Olympics and All Rights Reserved.

> Special Olympics is an international program of year-round sports training and athletic competition for children and adults with mental retardation. One million Special Olympics athletes in 150 countries around the world take part in more than 20,000 competitions each year.
>
> Special Olympics got its start in 1968 when Eunice Kennedy Shriver organized the First International Special Olympics Games at Soldier Field in Chicago, Illinois, USA. Shriver, who started a day camp for people with mental retardation in the early 1960s, saw that individuals with mental retardation were far more capable in sports and physical activities than many experts thought.
>
> Children and adults who participate in Special Olympics benefit from improved physical fitness and motor skills, greater self-confidence, a more positive self-image, friendships and increased family support. Special Olympics athletes carry these benefits with them

into their daily lives at home, in the classroom, on the job and in the community.

Special Olympics is committed to empowering people with mental retardation on and off the playing field. In addition to athletic competitions, Special Olympics offers athletes the chance to learn and grow as coaches, officials, spokespeople and leaders; improve athletes' health and fitness; and encourage school-age youth to break down barriers of prejudice and ignorance and celebrate differences.

Special Olympics could not have been created and would not exist today without the time, energy, dedication and commitment of more than 500,000 Special Olympics volunteers, including students, senior citizens, business people, family members of athletes, amateur and professional athletes and coaches, teachers and more. Anyone can be a Special Olympics volunteer, and benefit from life-long friendships and rewards of immeasurable value.

Today, Special Olympics is reaching out to the 170 million individuals with mental retardation around the world. The movement is committed to doubling the number of athletes involved in Special Olympics to 2 million by 2005. To learn more, visit **www. specialolympics.org**.

31.—THE AMERICAN RED CROSS
WWW.REDCROSS.ORG

We have all hear of the Red Cross. It's mission is: "The American Red Cross, a humanitarian organization led by volunteers and guided by its Congressional Charter and the Fundamental Principles of the International Red Cross Movement, will provide relief to victims of disasters and help people prevent, prepare for, and respond to emergencies." And their fundamental principles listed on their web site are: humanity, impartiality, neutrality, independence, voluntary service, unity, and universality. The Red Cross needs donations from us.

From the web site:

Here is a list of all the services that the Red Cross provides:

Armed Forces Emergency Services
Emergency Communication Services
Emergency Financial Assistance
Counseling
Services for Veterans
Community-Based Military Personnel
Local Resources
Military/Red Cross Partnership
References
You Can Help
News & Profiles
FAQs

Health and Safety Services
Courses for Your Community
Swimming and Lifeguarding
HIV/AIDS Education
Programs for Youth
Living Well/Living Safely
Resources
News & Profiles
FAQs

International Services
Global Issues
Emergency Disaster Response
Helping Our Red Cross Partners

Biomedical Services
Blood Services
Tissue Services
Plasma Services
National Testing Labs
Latest Research
News & Profiles
FAQs

Community Services
Food and Nutrition
Homeless
Transportation
Seniors
Lifeline
Hospitals/Nursing Homes
Youth
Helping in Other Ways
News & Profiles
FAQs

Disaster Services
Be Prepared
Keep Your Family Safe
After a Disaster
Educator's Information
Foreign Language Materials
About Us
Our Partners
News & Profiles
FAQs

Feeding Programs
Primary Health Care Programs
Tracing and Red Cross Messages
Geneva Conventions
Community Projects and Courses
Opportunities
News & Profiles
FAQs

Nursing
Nurse Enrollment
Student Nurses
History
Jane Delano Society
Links
News & Profiles
FAQs

Youth Involvement
Kids
Teens
Young Adults & College
Educators
News & Profiles
FAQs

Volunteering
Volunteer Philosophy
Join our Next Million Volunteers
Volunteer Opportunities Checklist
Awards and Recognition
Share Your Stories
FAQs

From the web site September 2002:

Amid Bells and Tributes, In New York, Red Cross President Helps Honor Victims of Sept. 11
*Written by **Cynthia Long**, Managing Editor, RedCross.org*

NEW YORK CITY, NY, Sept. 11, 2002—Shortly following the moment of silence at 8:46 a. m., a single bell tolled at 9:03 to mark the time the second jet hit the World Trade Center. The same bell tolled at 9:58, when the South Tower collapsed. And at 10:29, when the North Tower fell, that same single bell was joined by the chiming peal of dozens of church bells that echoed through the streets of Lower Manhattan and wafted into the commemoration ceremony at Ground Zero.

Families gathered at Ground Zero on Sept. 11, 2002, to pay tribute to loved ones killed one year ago.
Photo courtesy of the *New York Daily News*.

The chorus of bells floating into the crowd ushered in a visible wave of grief, as if the marking of this last terrible moment that occurred a year ago was providing those gathered with a release for their raw emotions.

As the tolling faded, the reading of the victims' names resumed. The name of each and every person who perished at the World Trade Center was read aloud by New York Mayor Michael Bloomberg, Governor George Pataki, firefighters, police officers, or a family member of someone who died at the site.

Among those reading the names was American Red Cross President and CEO Marsha Evans. She stood at the podium with a family member who lost a loved one at the World Trade Center. Alternating turns, they honored approximately 30 victims by reading their full names into the microphone.

"Witnessing and being part of this event is, without a doubt, the single most moving experience I have ever had," Evans said. "It was so powerful to be up at the podium and to see everyone gathered there, family members, friends and others affected by September 11th, all bonded together in such a strong, emotional way—the connection was palpable."

Evans visited the relief tents surrounding the perimeter of the ceremony to meet and support the hundreds of Red Cross volunteers providing mental health counseling, water, refreshments, and even much-needed tissues to those who had come to the service.

"The tireless work I see going on here is further confirmation that the Red Cross is always on the scene to help—here in New York and in cities and towns across the nation," Evans said. "We're there for the lesser known disasters, the house fires that affect a single family in the middle of the night that don't generate headlines and we're there for the unprecedented and unimaginable events that impact our entire country, like the tragedies we mark today."

The entire city is commemorating the anniversary with events like religious ceremonies, candlelight vigils, poetry readings, photographic exhibits and concerts. The common theme that seems to run through all the memorial events is that the city was hurt by the attacks, but not beaten. And as it heals, it is stronger than ever.

According to Evans, it is a theme that resonates throughout America as well. "We can maintain and build upon that strength through preparedness. Every person, every family, every business, every community should be actively taking steps toward emergency and disaster preparedness," she said. "Now more than ever-especially as the country is on a heightened alert status-emergency service and governmental organizations must work together to anticipate and plan for community needs in the event of a disaster. But people also need to prepare themselves by doing things like taking a first aid and CPR class, or developing a family disaster plan."

As the new head of the Red Cross, Evans hopes to take the message of preparedness to communities around the country and to underscore its importance among the Red Cross chapters that form the backbone of the organization.

"I've been here just five weeks, but I am already so proud to be part of this organization, to see people coming together to serve their fellow Americans here in New York, and to know that our volunteers are giving of themselves all over the country," Evans said. "Their service is the most wonderful reflection of what is so great about this country."

32.—MERCY SHIPS WWW.MERCYSHIPS.ORG

Our friends Jim and Patti have been good friends ever since we used to attend AYSO (American Youth Soccer Organization) meetings together some fifteen years ago. When they responded to our question as what is their favorite charity: Mercy Ships!
I might have guessed. Almost every year recently they have invited us to share a weekend or so on whatever boat they have that year. First a nice motorboat. Than a larger motorboat. I think that may have happened more than once until they changed to a sailboat. It was a very nice boat as well, with room to live and invite friends to stay over. So, not surprising to hear from them that when they retire they are planning to work with Mercy Ships. What a way to get an even larger boat! The *Anastasis* is a 522 ft. ship!

Mercy Ships currently has three ships that they operate as relief vessels that sail to areas of natural disaster and/or chronic need. They deliver supplies, provide surgical operations, treatments in mobile medical and dental clinics..

From the web site:

Mission

Mercy Ships brings hope and healing to the poor and needy around the world, primarily through ocean-going vessels, providing medical care, relief, development, and education.

Vision

Mercy Ships aims to serve one million people annually by 2004.

Values

1. We love God.

2. We love and serve people.

3. We are people of integrity.

4. We are committed to excellence in all we do.

33.—PLANNED PARENTHOOD— WWW.PLANNEDPARENTHOOD.ORG

I have not been involved much with planned parenthood, pro life, or pro choice. I do have some opinions. I do think that having one's own children, naturally or adopted, is a gift to be taken with joy and care. Raising children is no easy task and has rewards beyond measure.

However, for those who have not had access to the resources to care for children or access to information about how to plan for children and have them more or less when you want to—I think Planned Parenthood has some very useful things to do.

From their web site: © PPFA

Planned Parenthood Federation of America, Inc., is the world's largest and most trusted voluntary reproductive health care organization. Founded by Margaret Sanger in 1916 as America's first birth control clinic, Planned Parenthood believes in everyone's right to choose when or whether to have a child, that every child should be wanted and loved, and that women should be in charge of their own destinies.

Mission Statement
A Reason for Being
Planned Parenthood believes in the fundamental right of each individual, throughout the world, to manage his or her fertility, regardless of the individual's income, marital status, race, ethnicity, sexual orientation, age, national origin, or residence. We believe that respect and value for diversity in all aspects of our organization are essential to our well-being. We believe that reproductive self-determination must be voluntary and preserve the individual's right to privacy. We further believe that such self-determination will contribute to an enhancement of the quality of life, strong family relationships, and population stability.

Based on these beliefs, and reflecting the diverse communities within which we operate, the mission of Planned Parenthood is:

- to provide comprehensive reproductive and complementary health care services in settings which preserve and protect the essential privacy and rights of each individual;

- to advocate public policies which guarantee these rights and ensure access to such services;

- to provide educational programs which enhance understanding of individual and societal implications of human sexuality;

- to promote research and the advancement of technology in reproductive health care and encourage understanding of their inherent bioethical, behavioral, and social implications.

[Adopted 1984; Revised 1995]

34.—FREE STREET PROGRAMS—WWW.FREESTREET.ORG

Every year for the past few years we have sent a few dollars to the "Free Street Programs" to support their work. We happen to know a person on the board of directors who we hold in high regard. That seems to insure that it is a worthwhile program.

From the web site:

Free Street Mission

Free Street Programs is an arts outreach organization that uses the performing arts to enhance the literacy, self-esteem, creativity and employability of populations consistently excluded from mainstream cultural programming.

Through workshops in writing, theater, music, and dance, Free Street develops performances and performing companies that educate and motivate participants on both sides of the stage to address the issues and aspirations of their communities.

Free Street opens the potential of youth through theater and writing so they practice being creative, active participants in their own destiny.

35.—AMERICARES (A CRITICAL CARE AMBULANCE FOR THE WORLD—SAYS BARBARA BUSH)— WWW.AMERICARES.ORG

The other day I opened my mail and there was a letter to me from Barbara Bush. Well, it wasn't exactly a personal letter but it did catch my attention as Barbara Bush seemed to be a first lady that was able to offend almost no one during her stay in the White House. I like Barbara. Her letter told the story of the beach that was littered with starfish that had been washed up and would die in the sun if not returned to the waves. A little boy was walking on the beach and picking up the starfish, one by one and tossing them back into the sea. An elderly man was watching the lad, and went to him and said, "Why are you doing this? Can't you see that there are literally millions of these these starfish dying here on the beach? What you are doing can not possible make a difference."

The boy looked at the man for a moment, reached down and picked up one of the starfish and gently returned it to the water. "I made a difference to this one." He said.

Barbara went on to tell me that she wears a little starfish pin to symbolize the difference that AmeriCares makes.

From the web site:

AmeriCares is a nonprofit disaster relief and humanitarian aid organization, which provides immediate response to emergency medical needs—and supports long-term healthcare programs—for all people around the world, irrespective of race, creed or political persuasion.

AmeriCares solicits donations of medicines, medical supplies and other relief materials from U.S. and international manufacturers, and delivers them quickly and efficiently to indigenous healthcare and welfare professionals in <u>137 countries</u> around the world.

Financial contributions from individuals, corporations and foundations are used to defray the cost of <u>AmeriCares' programs</u>. Since its inception in 1982, AmeriCares has delivered more than $2.9 billion worth of life-saving supplies to those in need.

36.—MOTHERS AGAINST DRUNK DRIVING—WWW.MADD.ORG

Who among us has not been affected either directly or at least indirectly by news stories of the tragedies caused by drunk drivers? I have been lucky that when I was younger and drank more I did not cause an accident to myself or others while under the influence. When this topic comes up I usually recall the night way back when—I was in College in a small town in Ohio. A dry town. So we had to drive to the neighboring taverns five or more miles away on two lane country roads. One particular night, after several bottles of beer, (I didn't even like it that much—but it seemed the thing to do was drink a bunch of it!) I headed for home. I still remember after turning south on Route 700 to make the last five mile run home I saw six lanes of road to choose from. In the back of my alcohol drenched brain I knew it was a two-lane road so I had to pick from the six to get a good lane! I recall deciding that if I just pick a lane somewhere in the middle of all those lanes I'd be all right. The strategy must have worked as I am here today typing on this computer and not buried back in Ohio after smacking into a big maple tree by the side of the road.
Today I do not drink and drive.

From the web site:

MADD is more than just moms—we're real people—dads, young people, and other concerned individuals who want to stop drunk driving, support the victims of this violent crime, and prevent underage drinking.

The mission of Mothers Against Drunk Driving is to stop drunk driving, support the victims of this violent crime, and prevent underage drinking.

Mothers Against Drunk Driving is a 501(c)(3) non-profit grass roots organization with more than 600 chapters nationwide. MADD is not a crusade against alcohol consumption. Our focus is to look for effective solutions to the drunk driving and underage drinking problems, while supporting those who have already experienced the pain of these senseless crimes. For more insight into MADD's efforts and services, check our **MADD Quick Profile**.

MADD's History

MADD was founded by a small group of California women in 1980 after a 13-year-old-girl was killed by a hit-and-run driver. He had been out of jail on bail for only two days for another hit-and-run drunk driving crash and had three previous drunk driving arrests and two convictions. He was allowed to plea bargain to vehicular manslaughter. Although he was sentenced to two years in prison, the judge allowed the offender to serve time in work camp and later a halfway house.

Since 1980, MADD has continued to grow and pursue the efforts initiated by its founders. MADD's National President became an elected position with specific term of office. Two-thirds of MADD's volunteer national Board of Directors is composed of representatives from local chapters.

For a more detailed history of MADD, check our "**20 Year of Making a Difference**" chronology.

Drunk Driving is Not an Accident

37.—Christian Appalachian Project—WWW.CHRISAPP.ORG

I have never yet spent time in the Appalachia that we hear and read about. What I've assimilated from outside sources is that there is a pocket (at least) of poverty and hopelessness that seems to not be able to cure itself without outside intervention. A hand up is often needed for those who have sunken in to a pit of some sort—like a pit of despair or poverty. So, I have made some donations to what is being done to assist the folks in Appalachia. Sometimes I have purchased a doormat or a Christmas wreath as a way of supporting a business that is being run to help the Appalachians help themselves. I'm thinking that these efforts are along the line of teaching a person to fish rather than simply feeding them.

From the web site:

Our Mission Statement
The Christian Appalachian Project is an interdenominational, non-profit Christian organization committed to serving people in need in Appalachia by providing physical, spiritual and emotional support through a wide variety of programs and services.

CAP's Beginnings
Father Ralph W. Beiting, a Roman Catholic priest born and raised in northern Kentucky began dreaming of helping the people of Appalachia help themselves out of poverty in 1946. As a seminarian, Father Beiting accompanied several priests as they went out to preach in the mountains of eastern Kentucky. The oldest of eleven children who grew up during the Great Depression, Father Beiting was no stranger to need, but the soul-shattering poverty he observed that summer planted the seeds of a vision that eventually became the Christian Appalachian Project.

38.—EASTER SEALS—HELP THOSE WITH DISABILITIES ACHIEVE INDEPENDENCE— WWW.EASTER-SEALS.ORG

I have been an Independent Business Owner affiliated with Quixtar for some time. Each year at the special seminar called Dream Night, an opportunity to support Easter Seals is presented. It always seems a good thing to support the research and assistance to people, especially kids, with disabilities. Since there are hundreds of thousands of us affiliated with Quixtar, our combined contributions make a big difference I'm sure.

From the web site: (Courtesy of **www.easter-seals.org**)

We've come a long way.
For more than 80 years, Easter Seals has helped people with disabilities in communities nationwide. From creating the first national voluntary agency to speak and act on behalf of children with disabilities in the 1920s, to leading the creation and implementation of the Americans with Disabilities Act in the 1990s, Easter Seals continues to be an integral part of life, helping more than a million people gain greater independence each year. One in every five Americans has a disability, and Easter Seals is there with expert help, hope and humanity.

The Story of Easter Seals

Easter Seals has been helping individuals with disabilities and special needs, and their families, live better lives for more than 80 years. Whether helping someone improve physical mobility, return to work or simply gain greater independence for everyday living, Easter Seals offers a variety of services to help people with disabilities address life's challenges and achieve personal goals.

Tragedy Leads to Inspiration

In 1907, Ohio-businessman Edgar Allen lost his son in a streetcar accident. The lack of adequate medical services available to save his son prompted Allen to sell his business and begin a fund-raising campaign to build a hospital in his hometown of Elyria, Ohio. Through this new hospital, Allen was surprised to learn that children with disabilities were often hidden from public view. Inspired by this discovery, in 1919 Allen founded what became known as the National Society for Crippled Children, the first organization of its kind.

The Birth of the Seal

In the spring of 1934, the organization launched its first Easter "seals" campaign to raise money for its services. To show their support, donors placed the seals on envelopes and letters. Cleveland Plain Dealer cartoonist J.H. Donahey designed the first seal. Donahey based the design on a concept of simplicity because those served by the charity asked "simply for the right to live a normal life."

The lily—a symbol of spring—was officially incorporated as Easter Seals' logo in 1952 for its association with resurrection and new life and has appeared on each seal since.

Easter Seals Emerges

The overwhelming public support for the Easter "seals" campaign triggered a nationwide expansion of the organization and a swell of grassroots efforts on behalf of people with disabilities. By 1967, the Easter "seal" was so well recognized, the organization formally adopted the name "Easter Seals."

39.—SALESIAN MISSIONS—
WWW.SALESIANMISSIONS.ORG

The mailings I've received form the Salesians have prompted me to send them money form time to time—they do good work I'm sure!

From the web site:

The Salesians
Who are the Salesians and what do they do? They're a "modern miracle", the famous Bishop Fulton Sheen once called them. From humble beginnings in the last century, the Salesians of Don Bosco have become one of three largest religious families of men and women in the Church. And from the beginning, Don Bosco wanted his family to be missionary in spirit. Follow the beginnings and the growth of the Salesian family to the present day. Understand Don Bosco himself and know what inspires the men and women who continue his work, his dream, his mission throughout the world. You'll see the who, the why, the where, the when. And we'll even show you each and every place where the Salesian Fathers, Brothers and Sisters are working today.

Around The World

Test your knowledge of geography while you browse the world of Salesian Missions. Travel from <u>Latin America</u> to <u>Asia</u>, <u>Africa</u>, the <u>Middle East</u>, <u>Europe</u>, <u>North America</u> and <u>Australia</u>. Click into the work of the Salesians and thousands of <u>cooperators</u>—in 122 countries of the world. You'll learn the "facts and figures" and many times, the encouraging story of lives touched and mended, of futures bright and promise-filled.

40.—MARYKNOLL—A MISSION OF HOPE AND HEALING— WWW.MARYKNOLL.ORG

Back a few years ago when I went to a run (10K, 5K, 10Mile, etc.) almost every weekend, there was a 10 mile run that started and ended at a facility that I think of every time I get a request from Maryknoll. The place I think of was a live-in facility for disabled individuals and we would see some of the residents on the grounds as we gathered for and finished the run. We ran to raise money for their support. I was glad to do it and it was also a great course for that run too. The course was roughly a large country block, mostly flat, but it included a couple memorable hills. The first hill was an out-and-back side loop off the rectangular main course. That loop was down going out and an uphill struggle coming back. Then to cap off the hill work, there was a sharp downhill just after the aforementioned side loop. That second down hill was steep enough to challenge our ability to let it all hang out—steep enough to make you think you might be getting out of control. Probably, that was where I ran faster than anywhere else in my life!

Now, it turns out that Maryknoll has nothing to do with the place where I ran in the aforementioned races, but for some reason the name reminds me of that place.

From the web site:

Maryknoll, The U.S. based Catholic mission movement includes: the Maryknoll Society (priests and brothers), Maryknoll Congregation (Sisters), the Maryknoll Mission Association of the Faithful (laity, priests and religious), and the Maryknoll Affiliates.

Since 1911, Catholics in the United States have responded to the worldwide cry of the poor by becoming Maryknoll Missioners. Today, Maryknollers help people overseas build communities of faith. Some work in war zones with refugees, others minister to the sick, the elderly, orphans or people with AIDS. Through lives of service, Maryknollers translate the gospel of love into different languages and in different cultures.

41.—MEDICINS SANS FRONTIERES—DOCTORS WITHOUT BORDERS— WWW.DOCTORSWITHOUT BORDERS.ORG

If you were a medical doctor, would you think it a good idea to give part of your time to people in other countries for whom access to medical treatment is out of the question? Out of the question except for those doctors who give their time through Doctors Without Borders. Probably most of those who give their time have families at home, bills to pay at home, and yet they see a way to share their expertise with people who might otherwise never get treatments that give them an improved quality of life or even life itself!
Doctors Without Borders won the Nobel Peace Prize in 1999!

From the web site:

What is Doctors Without Borders/Médecins Sans Frontières (MSF)?

Providing Medical Relief Worldwide
Médecins Sans Frontières (also known as Doctors Without Borders or MSF) delivers emergency aid to victims of armed conflict, epidemics, and natural and man-made disasters, and to others who lack health care due to social or geographical isolation.
MSF was founded in 1971 by a small group of French doctors who believed that all people have the right to medical care and that the needs of these people supersede respect for national borders. It was the first non-governmental organization to both provide emergency medical assistance and publicly bear witness to the plight of the populations they served.

A private, nonprofit organization, MSF is at the forefront of emergency health care as well as care for populations suffering from endemic diseases and neglect. MSF provides primary health care, performs surgery, rehabilitates hospitals and clinics, runs nutrition and sanitation programs, trains local medical personnel, and provides mental health care. Through longer-term programs, MSF treats chronic diseases such as tuberculosis, malaria, sleeping sickness, and AIDS; assists with the medical and psychological problems of marginalized populations including street children and ethnic minorities; and brings health care to remote, isolated areas where resources and training are limited.

MSF unites direct medical care with a commitment to bearing witness and speaking out against the underlying causes of suffering. Its volunteers protest violations of humanitarian law on behalf of populations who have no voice, and bring the concerns of their patients to public forums, such as the United Nations, governments, and the media. In a wide range of circumstances, MSF volunteers have spoken out against atrocities they have witnessed—from Chechnya, to Angola, to Kosovo. MSF is an international network with sections in 18 countries. Each year, more than 2,000 volunteer doctors, nurses, other medical professionals, logistics experts, water/sanitation engineers, and administrators join 15,000 locally hired staff to provide medical aid in more than 80 countries.

Logistical Expertise

MSF has built a strong logistical capability to support its medical expertise, enabling its volunteers to work in the most remote or unstable parts of the world. Teams arrive at a project site with prepackaged medical kits so they can begin working immediately. Custom-designed by MSF for specific field situations, geographic conditions, and climates, a kit may contain a complete surgical theater, for example, or all the supplies needed to treat hundreds of cholera patients. MSF kits have been replicated by relief organizations worldwide.

Bearing Witness and Speaking Out

"We are by nature an organization that is unable to tolerate indifference. We hope that by arousing awareness and a desire to understand, we will also stir up indignation and stimulate action."—Rony Brauman, MD, Former President, MSF

Bearing witness to the plight of populations at risk is part of MSF's mission, in the United States and worldwide. Whether giving testimony at the United Nations or conducting an educational campaign aimed at schoolchildren, the organization works to raise awareness of the plight of the populations it serves. Through its Access to Essential Medicines Campaign, MSF is confronting the difficulties faced by people in the developing world in obtaining affordable, effective treatments for infectious diseases. The organization has also launched public education projects to raise awareness of the trauma faced by children in a war zone, the devastation caused by malnutrition, and the plight of refugees.

Volunteerism

MSF is an organization based on volunteerism. In helping to relieve the suffering of others, the MSF volunteer not only gives freely of his or her humanity, but creates a link of solidarity from his or her home country to a population in need. At times the sole international witness to a crisis situation, the MSF volunteer plays a critical role in the communities where he or she works. It is the independent nature of the volunteer's commitment that gives special legitimacy to the testimony provided by MSF and that ensures the organization's continued dynamism.

Financial Independence

To maintain its operational independence and flexibility, MSF relies on the general public for the majority of its operating funds. Other financial support is provided by foundations, corporations, nonprofit organizations, the U.S. and other governments, and international agencies. The MSF international network collectively strives to direct at least 80 percent of its expenditures to program activities.

42.—FEED THE CHILDREN—
WWW.FEEDTHECHILDREN.ORG

Feed the Children is one of many NGOs that collect money and put it to good use. This organization was founded by a man after visiting Haiti and seeing an unmet need.

From the web site:

Our Mission Statement
Feed The Children is a nonprofit, Christian, charitable organization providing physical, spiritual, educational, vocational/technical, psychological, economic and medical assistance and other necessary aid to children, families, and persons in need in the United States and internationally.

What We Do
During our 22-year history, Feed The Children has created and developed one of the world's largest private organizations dedicated to feeding hungry people. Last year, Feed The Children shipped 61 million pounds of food and 34 million pounds of other essentials to children and families in all 50 states and in 41 foreign countries. Feed The Children supplements 670,000 meals a day, worldwide.
Our system is fast and efficient. We deliver the food to some 4,200-partner organizations that speed it to over 50,000 other groups who work with the hungry. **The food is provided at no cost to recipients.**

International Outreach
Feed The Children's international programs consist of four components:

• Feeding

• Development/Self-help

- Medical

- Emergency Relief

We provide clothing, medical assistance and educational opportunities to underprivileged children in 85 nations around the world. Through schools, orphanages and church-related feeding programs, Feed The Children touched the lives of thousands of children overseas. We send shipments to Africa, the Caribbean, Central America, South America, Southeast Asia, the Middle East, Eastern Europe and the former Soviet Union Republic where direct distribution is made to recipients. Additionally, we provide financial assistance to orphanages, schools and other charitable groups in these regions.

A key goal is to help needy families move beyond relief assistance and become productive and self-sufficient members of their community. Through long-term, self-help development programs funded by grants and by our Child Sponsorship partners, tens of thousands of families in foreign lands have increased their earning potential through new, marketable skills.

Medical Team
Our **medical team** travels to third world countries with volunteer doctors, nurses, dentists and other support personnel. The teams perform minor surgery, treat diseases and injuries, and provide much-needed medicine. Our eye clinic provides optical exams and glasses.

A Brief History
Feed The Children was founded by Larry Jones, who serves as President. During a trip to Haiti in 1979, Larry witnessed acute misery and needless hunger. Such overwhelming needs, coupled with Larry's knowledge of enormous food and grain surpluses in America, led Larry and his wife, Frances, to create Feed The Children.

A Few Achievements
Feed The Children's achievements are widely noted:

- In 2000 Larry and Frances Jones received the H. J. Heimlich Humanitarian Award for their humanitarian relief efforts throughout the world.

- In 1995, *The Chronicle of Philanthropy* ranked Feed The Children as America's 5th largest international relief and development organization.

- Based on private donor support, *U. S. News and World Report* ranked Feed The Children as the third largest U. S. charity involved in global aid.

...approximately 90% of our total budget goes directly to programs.

43.—OVERSEAS DEVELOPMENT INSTITUTE—WWW.ID21.ORG

A woman who used to work for Childreach (see #4) and who now works for Oxfam (see #5), sent me an article from this organization based in the UK.

Overseas Development Institute
Portland House,
Stag Place,
London SW1E 5DP, UK

From the web site:

About ID21

ID21 is a fast-track research reporting service backed by the UK Department for International Development. It aims to make policy-makers and on-the-ground development managers aware of the latest and best in British development research findings. Online, in print and through the Southern media, ID21 showcases fresh and unusual research angles on major development issues. More, it offers intelligent lessons for all who strive to make development succeed in future.

What you get

- free access to an online database loaded with searchable digests of up-to-date research touching international development concerns and dilemmas worldwide

- the combined knowledge of some 40 university research departments and think-tanks, as well as researchers in the private consultant and voluntary sectors

- non-partisan, one-page Research Highlights, free of jargon and framed to be read by professionals in the business of shaping or implementing development policy

- e-mail addresses, other direct contact details, hotlinks and printed sources, to ease the direct flow of knowledge and advice between researcher and research user.

The ID21 Online selection process is guided by a network of academic advisors and all entries are also seen and approved by originators, a double check on quality and reliability. Source materials include conference papers, research newsletters and other 'grey' or pre-publication materials. But work of more than two years' vintage, literature reviews, highly theoretical studies and institutional policy or position statements are normally excluded.

About ID21

ID21 is a fast-track research reporting service backed by the UK Department for International Development. It aims to make policy-makers and on-the-ground development managers aware of the latest and best in British development research findings. Online, in print and through the Southern media, ID21 showcases fresh and unusual research angles on major development issues. More, it offers intelligent lessons for all who strive to make development succeed in future.

What you get

- free access to an online database loaded with searchable digests of up-to-date research touching international development concerns and dilemmas worldwide

- the combined knowledge of some 40 university research departments and think-tanks, as well as researchers in the private consultant and voluntary sectors

- non-partisan, one-page Research Highlights, free of jargon and framed to be read by professionals in the business of shaping or implementing development policy

- e-mail addresses, other direct contact details, hotlinks and printed sources, to ease the direct flow of knowledge and advice between researcher and research user.

The ID21 Online selection process is guided by a network of academic advisors and all entries are also seen and approved by originators, a double check on quality and reliability. Source materials include conference papers, research newsletters and other 'grey' or pre-publication materials. But work of more than two years' vintage, literature reviews, highly theoretical studies and institutional policy or position statements are normally excluded.

44.—THE NATURE CONSERVANCY— WWW.NATURECONSERVANCY.ORG

Someone needs to be concerned about how we treat our planet. So far it is the only one we know how to live on and we need to be sure we don't mess up the living space!

Every family in order to stay healthy needs to keep their living quarters clean and neat and in good repair. The same applies to the human family that inhabits this beautiful earth! The Nature Conservancy is one organization formed to help keep the planet in good shape.

From the web site:

Our Mission
The mission of The Nature Conservancy is to preserve the plants, animals and natural communities that represent the diversity of life on Earth by protecting the lands and waters they need to survive.

About Us
The Nature Conservancy, a nonprofit organization founded in 1951, is the world's largest private international conservation group. Working with communities, businesses and people like you, we protect millions of acres of valuable lands and waters worldwide. View our Annual Report.

Our Conservation Approach
The Nature Conservancy uses Conservation by Design as its framework for mission success. Our conservation approach includes: · Setting priorities through ecoregional planning; · Developing strategies to conserve both single and multiple conservation areas; · Taking direct conservation action; and · Measuring conservation success.

Our Commitment
Through sound science, tangible results and a non-confrontational approach, The Nature Conservancy expands the boundaries of conservation to save the Earth's Last Great Places for future generations.

45.—PHYSICIANS FOR SOCIAL RESPONSIBILITY—WWW.PSR.ORG

Here is a group of physicians who have taken it upon themselves to make a difference. By promoting socially responsible behavior by our companies and corporations and other organizations that may have a tendency to avoid social responsibility in the actions they take and/or the products they produce these physicians are involved at a higher level than what they might accomplish from their individual practices.

From the web site:

Physicians for Social Responsibility represents more than 20,000 physicians, nurses and health care professionals devoted to nuclear disarmament, violence prevention and environmental health.

Understanding that nuclear war continues to be the most acute threat to human life and the global biosphere, PSR reaffirms its commitment of nearly forty years to the elimination of nuclear weapons and the reversal of the arms race and the national budgetary priorities which fuel that race, sacrificing our nation's health, social and economic needs.

With a reduction in East-West tensions, PSR sees a chance for our nation to address more insidious environmental threats to human survival, such as global warming, ozone depletion, toxic chemicals, and the world population explosion.

Recognizing that neglect of social problems and emphasis on militarism has resulted in a crisis of societal violence, PSR also seeks to reverse our domestic arms race and to encourage ways of finding peaceful solutions to interpersonal and local disputes, as well as international conflicts.

MISSION

Physicians for Social Responsibility is committed to the elimination of nuclear and other weapons of mass destruction, the achievement of a sustainable environment, and the reduction of violence and its causes.

VALUES

In the ancient and universal tradition of the physician who promotes healing and seeks truth, members subscribe to the following values:

- That life on Earth is precious, powerful and vulnerable;

- That human life draws vital sustenance and coherence from the ecological and social systems in which it participates;

- That the acquisition and application of scientific knowledge imposes the responsibility to protect life, not to endanger or destroy it;

- That knowledge about global threats results from experience and scientific study including modeling and simulation, which inherently contain uncertainty;

- That the necessary decisions based on such uncertainties must be evaluated in settings open to public review, so that the best possible approaches can be achieved;

- That citizens have a right to informed participation in such decision-making processes made by both government and industry which affect their health, welfare and environment; and

- That our commitment to future generations requires that problems of violence and militarism, global environmental degradation and social and economic inequities be addressed now and not be left as a toxic legacy to be solved by those who follow us.

THEMES

Four major themes infuse the work of PSR:

1) A commitment to democratic political processes and traditions.
2) An affirmation of the physician's role as a teacher.
3) A belief that as physicians and teachers, as we empower our students and patients to choose healthy life-styles and caring interactions, we can also convince people and nations to choose policies which contribute to ourcommon health and security.
4) Promotion of the physical and psychological health and well-being of humanity.

As individuals and as citizens, we respect and support these tenets of our society: a tolerance for diversity, a capacity to live and let live, an insistence on fairness, and an abiding respect for individual rights.

As members of the medical community committed to the promotion of global health, it is our obligation to share with all of humanity our understanding that eliminating weapons of mass destruction, preserving a sustainable environment and reducing interpersonal violence and its causes are the most realistic strategies for assuring global survival.

46.—CAMPAIGN FOR A LANDMINE FREE WORLD—VIETNAM VETERANS OF AMERICA FOUNDATION— WWW.VVAF.ORG

(see #66, 67, 68, and 69)

Here again is a Veterans organization working to achieve a better world for all of us. How many landmines have been left out there in the countryside where there was conflict. How many times have you seen or heard about children and others being blown up or losing limbs from these mines. Shouldn't we have a landmine free world?

From the web site:

VVAF's Campaign for a Landmine Free World has, for more than a decade, worked to raise awareness about the suffering and devastation caused by landmines by advocating for a global ban on all landmines. The worldwide anti-landmine movement co-founded by VVAF president Bobby Muller in 1991 grew into the International Campaign to Ban Landmines and led to the Ottawa Treaty banning antipersonnel landmines and to the Nobel Peace Prize, both in 1997. In addition, VVAF supports efforts to **locate and remove existing mines** and provides desperately needed medical and rehabilitative services to landmine victims and other survivors of conflict in seven war-ravaged countries.

Long after conflicts end and treaties are signed, landmines continue to kill and maim innocent civilians. In fact, each year more than 18,000 men, women, and children lose arms, legs, even their lives to landmines. Hundreds of mines may lie hidden between villagers' homes and their sources of food and water, forcing them to risk their lives each day or face certain death by hunger or thirst. And, ironically, **landmines are no longer even an effective weapon of war.**

VVAF has fitted hundreds of thousands of prosthetic limbs in countries around the world, and we continue to provide rehabilitation to the victims, as well as periodic repairs to the limbs. Adapting to the needs, conditions and resources of each country where we are at work, our programs also provide patients with job training and employment, helping them regain independence and self-respect as well as mobility. Our own experiences have taught us that rehabilitating war victims means more than rebuilding their bodies; it also means helping them rebuild their lives.

Concerts for a Landmine Free World bring together on stage some of the most distinguished voices and finest singers-songwriters of our time to share songs and stories and help raise public awareness about the global landmine tragedy. Many of the artists who give of their time and resources to help VVAF have traveled overseas to tour our rehabilitation clinics, meet with international staff and clinic patients and experience first-hand how silk scarves are hand-woven on wooden looms at the **Preah Vihear clinic** in northern Cambodia. The family of musicians who today champion the landmine cause was formed in 1998 by Grammy Award winner Emmylou Harris, following her trip with VVAF President Bobby Muller to Cambodia and Vietnam.

- **Toward a Mine-free Military**-Recent VVAF briefings of high-level civilian and military leaders on what we have learned about landmines indicate growing credibility and acceptance of the following points:

  - Landmines had no tactical or strategic significance in the Gulf War;

  - The U.S. military has no plans to use its landmine stocks in the initial defense of U.S. troops in Korea;

  - The U.S. military has better alternative weapons and doctrine to meet any envisioned threat; and

- Landmines can be replaced with lighter, more lethal, and smarter antipersonnel and anti-armor weapons, reasserting U.S. leadership on the landmine issue.

47.—Do a Good Deed, Or Three!—

In late 2002 on a trip to the grocery store I entered the checkout line behind a woman who was unloading her very full cart from in front of it. I said, "Excuse me, do you mind if I unload the things from the back of your cart?" It was pretty clear she couldn't reach all those things without climbing over something. She looked back at me and replied, "Oh thanks, are you doing your good deed for today?" That led to a conversation about good deeds. She told me she had been doing three good deeds every day since she was about 20 or for 15 years or more. She now had a nine year old son and she had him enrolled in the process too. They often competed when they both spotted an opportunity to perform a good deed.

So, what if we all took on this good deed challenge?

48.—FIND THE KIDS
WWW.FINDTHEKIDS.ORG

One afternoon I was waiting for my wife to call with which train to meet. When the phone rang I didn't go check caller ID to screen out telemarketers, I picked it right up.

Well, it was a telemarketer, not actually selling a product but asking for money to support the cause of finding lost or kidnapped kids. I corrected the guy's pronunciation of the name of our town as a way to make his next call more effective but told him I was not donating to that charity today. However, before he got off the line it occurred to me that the organization might deserve a place in this book. So I asked him for the web site.

When I told him about the book he agreed it belongs—why wouldn't he? So I checked it out.

When I was talking to Eric, from Vancouver, I first asked him on whose behalf he was calling. "I represent the Xentel company" he told me. Well, then he started talking about the pictures of missing kids on milk cartons and such. Then when he told me the web site, **www.findthekids.org** I wondered what happened to the name Xentel.

If you look below at what I've copied for you from the web site you'll see. Xentel is actually the name of a telemarketing company that the "Committee for Missing Children" hires to raise funds. You will also see that if you want your donations to go straight to the cause, don't respond to Xentel, just send your money straight to the cause headquarters—you will find them on the web site.

From the web site: www.findthekids.org

OUR MISSION

First and foremost, we are a parent advocacy group. We assist parents by providing the help they deserve and ensuring that their rights are protected.

Through the dedication of our photo partners, we produce and distribute billions of images of missing children worldwide.

We gather and share information, serve as a clearinghouse for information and the laws about missing children, and are developing the largest database in this country on missing children.

UNDERSTANDING OUR MISSION

The first phase of our mission deals with parent advocacy. We want to ensure that parents of missing and abducted children receive all the help they deserve and that the rights of parents are protected Today there are no laws that give a parent control over the search for their own children. In fact many parents do not even have the right to see the information collected on their own children. In some cases parents are required to send in a îfreedom of informationî request to see what has been collected by the vary agencies set up to help them. In many cases parents end up looking for their own children, and they have to do it themselves if they want to get it done. In November, 1995, The Committee for Missing Children brought together a group of parents of missing children to form the first-ever parent advocacy group. Again in August, 1999 the Committee brought together 25 parents and 37 agencies and professionals to develop a handbook/reference guide for parents of missing and abducted children. In May 2000, we held a meeting of parents and professionals in Langenselbold, Germany where we maintain an office. Our goal was, and continues to be, to bring together all parents of missing and previously missing children. Only then will these parents start to develop the clout needed to force law enforcement, local, state, and Federal officials, to recognize their plight.

Second, we are a photo distributor. Our objective is to distribute as many pictures of missing children as we can. We do this by encouraging educational dealers, manufacturers and publishers to produce pages of missing children and distributing them throughout the country. The Committee for Missing Children has become a leader in the area of family abductions. Along with our photo partners, we have printed over two billion images, representing over 1,500 missing children. These pictures go into the schools by several means. Catalogs, inserts, box stuffers, etc. It is our conclusion that most family-abducted children will eventually end up enrolled in school. Through our poster program we have distributed pictures, both domestically and internationally, of stranger-abducted children, Family-abducted children and endangered runaways. Through a distribution program with the National Center for Missing and Exploited Children, our posters were placed in all Wal-Mart stores and Sam's Clubs. We have found that although one out of six children is located through photo distribution, we want to increase the odds.

The last phase of our mission is information gathering. It is our objective to be a clearinghouse for information on missing and abducted children as well as the laws that govern the missing children field. We will also file and disseminate case histories that deal with both domestic and internationally abducted children. The Committee for Missing Children, Inc. is in the process of developing the largest database in the United States on missing children. This database will be available to parents of missing children, other non-profit child-find groups, both domestic and international, and local, state, and national agencies that deal with missing children.

If you click on "donations" you'll find the following:

100% of all donations made directly to the Committee For Missing Children, Inc. goes for programs

The Committee for Missing Children, Inc. uses the following telemarketing firms: LAS (Part of Civic Development Group) Xentel, Inc. and All Pro Telemarketing Corp. In addition we have an agreement with The Vehicle Donation Processing Center, Inc. The amount of money we receive from each of the above varies.

We feel that we have some of the best telemarkerers working for us, however there are times that things may not always go as we would like. If for any reason you feel that you were not treated properly or you have additional questions for us or our telemarketers, please contact me directly at 678-376-6265 or by E-mail at **findthekids@ compuserve.com**. You may also write to me at The Committee for Missing Children, Inc. 242 Stone Mountain Street, Lawrenceville, GA 30045
David C. Thelen, CEO

Section IV
Support Efforts Focused on Native American Issues

49.—CHRISTIAN RELIEF SERVICES—RUNNING STRONG FOR AMERICAN INDIAN YOUTH— WWW.CHRISTIANRELIEF.ORG

The thing that got me to donate regularly to this organization is Billy Mills. Billy won the gold medal at the Olympics many years ago. He was one of the first Native Americans to win at the Olympics for the USSA. He wasn't expected to win. He simply put his whole heart into the race, it was the 10K, and couldn't be beat! So when Billy asks me for money I am inspired to send some. They also keep sending me gifts! Most recently, an umbrella. For some reason I like to have umbrellas.

From the web site:

Christian Relief Services connects the vast resources of America through collaboration and partnership formed with grass roots charitable groups, churches and human service agencies, empowers local volunteers to help those in need in their own communities and enables people to help themselves.

Billy Mills: Running Strong for American Indian Youth® (a project of Christian Relief Services) Spokesperson and Olympic Champion

"Your life is a gift from the Creator. Your gift back to the Creator is what you do with your life."—Billy Mills

Olympic Champion, Billy Mills, serves as Running Strong's National Spokesperson, encouraging Native youth with his message based on character, dignity and pride. He plays an integral role in our youth programs and is an invaluable resource with our work in Indian country. In Lakota culture, someone who has achieved success would have a 'giveaway' to thank the support system of family and friends who helped him achieve his goal. Billy's work with Running Strong is his way of giving something back to American Indian people.

50.—NATIVE AMERICAN HERITAGE ASSOCIATION— WWW.NAHA-INC.ORG

Somehow the Rose Bud and Pine Ridge Native American Reservations got my address and phone number and have kept me on their mailing list for a few years. They collect donations to help take care of the people on the reservations. It seems the need continues.

And, it seems there is a lot we can learn from the Native American's culture that pre-dates our non-Native (primarily European based) North American culture.

From the web site:

Almost everyday, somewhere on the reservation, there is a funeral and there is a <u>Giveaway</u> to honor someone who died one year before. But, thanks to NAHA, there is a huge amount of hope being delivered with every truckload of nutritious food items. No one makes a trip out here without extra water, food, and gasoline if you can afford it. You need to carry a flashlight, blankets, and some form of communication; however, there are places out here in Indian Country where neither cell phones or CB radios work.

51.—COUNCIL OF INDIAN NATIONS— WWW.CINPROGRAMS.ORG

I receive requests from several native American organizations. This one represents many tribes in the South West part of the US. Council of Indian Nations is a program of The National Relief Charities, **www.nrcprograms.org** that includes other program members also.

From the web site:

The Council of Indian Nations assists American Indians living in remote reservation communities in the Southwest United States
Our mission: to help Native American people improve the quality of their lives by providing opportunities for them to bring about positive changes in their communities.

Southwest Indian People
(Northern Tribes)

- Apache

- Navajo

- Hopi

- Pueblo People

- Southern Paiute

(Colorado River Tribes)

- Havasupai

- Hualapai

- Mohave

- Yuma, Cocopah, and Maricopa

(Central/Southern Arizona Tribes)

- Papago

- Pima

- Yaqui

- Yavapai

Southwest Indian History

- Early History

- 300 BC

  - Anasazi

  - Hohokam

  - Mogollon

- 1500 AD

- 1600 AD

- 1845 to Present

Southwest Indians Today

- Housing

- Education

- Economics

- Health

52.—RED CLOUD INDIAN SCHOOL— WWW.REDCLOUDSCHOOL.ORG

This organization represents Native Americans in South Dakota. My donation went to the education of 600 Oglala Lakota Sioux students on the Pine Ridge Reservation. The vision of Red Cloud Indian School is on of educational excellence within a context of true caring.

From the web site:

Mission Statement:

The mission of Red Cloud Indian School—Holy Rosary Mission, a Catholic Institution administered by the Jesuits and the Lakota People, is to develop and grow as a vibrant Church, through an education of the mind and spirit that promotes the values of the Lakota Culture.

About Red Cloud Indian School:

Red Cloud Indian School (Grades K-12) was founded as Holy Rosary Mission in 1888 by the Jesuits at the request Chief Red Cloud, of the Oglala Sioux Indians residing on the Pine Ridge Reservation. Chief Red Cloud had continually petitioned the government to allow the "Blackrobes" (Jesuits) to come to the reservation in order to establish a school. His continual efforts brought about the development and existence of Holy Rosary Mission.

Holy Rosary Church was built on the site chosen by Chief Red Cloud and the first Jesuits to arrive on the Pine Ridge Reservation. Construction of the brick and stone structure began in 1896 and was completed in time for Christmas Day Mass in 1898.

The Church was a major part of the experiences and memories of generations of Lakota men, women, and children who passed through its doors. It was the home parish for many people in the area. In addition, due to its existence as a boarding school and the presence of students involved in Jesuit education, the Church had deep roots in the lives of people throughout the Pine Ridge Reservation and beyond.

The basic design of the building reflected the westward movement of the Buffalo Mission German Jesuits from northern New York state. It was the first brick country church west of the Missouri River, and all of its bricks were made by hand. The building included 28 imported stained glass windows and the alters of the church were all hand carved wood. The craftsmen built a church of bricks, mortar, and above all, artistry and love.

In later years, 15 parishes were added to serve different geographic locations on the reservation, and Our Lady of Lourdes, a second elementary school, was established to help meet the needs of the northern end of the Pine Ridge Reservation. Our Lady of Lourdes is located 15 miles north of the historic site at Wounded Knee. Please read some **facts about Pine Ridge**.

53.—THE SMITHSONIAN'S NATIONAL MUSEUM OF THE AMERICAN INDIAN— <u>WWW.SI.EDU/NMAI</u>

Here is another organization formed to support the Native Americans by creating a museum to honor them.

From the web site:

Welcome from Rick West
As founding director of the National Museum of the American Indian, I have had the opportunity and honor of visiting a multitude of significant Native places throughout the Western Hemisphere-from the American Southwest and Hawaii, to Canada, to South and Central America. Native people are profoundly connected to their origins, the places they come from. These places are the source of community identity and cultural continuity.

At NMAI, we think of our new museum on the National Mall, set to open in 2004, along with our other sites (the Cultural Resources Center in Suitland, Maryland, and the George Gustav Heye Center in New York), as Native places of a kind. We hope that visitors to our buildings will find not only a wealth of cultural knowledge and aesthetic wonders, but a welcoming spirit as well.

In a similar way, we hope that visitors to our Web site will also feel that they are in a Native place, be it one situated in virtual, as opposed to physical, space. It is our fervent wish that by visiting our home on the Internet, you will experience something of the unique nature and welcoming spirit of the National Museum of the American Indian.

Rick West
(Southern Cheyenne and member of the Cheyenne and Arapaho Tribes of Oklahoma)

54.—St. Labre Indian School— WWW.STLABRE.ORG

This is another organization supporting the needs of Native Americans who live in our midst and somehow do not enjoy the economic freedom that many of us who are really immigrants enjoy. So, in Montana, where the Cheyenne and Crow Indians were pushed off the lands they had lived on for generations by homesteaders in the late 1800s, the St. Labre Indian School was founded to be a refuge for America's first truly homeless people.

From the web site:

Who we are
St. Labre is a Native American Catholic school located along the banks of the Tongue River in southeastern Montana which provides educational opportunities to the Northern Cheyenne and Crow people. St. Labre operates four schools with a total enrollment of approximately 700 students.

How it all began
St. Labre began as a result of one soldier's concern for the Northern Cheyenne. George Yoakam, an ex-soldier, had been helping the Northern Cheyenne in settling the region. He contacted Montana Bishop John Brondel and told him of Indian people who were roaming the Tongue River Valley without homes or land—a reservation had not been set aside as yet. Land was purchased by the Bishop and on March 29, 1884, St. Labre Indian School became a reality.

In response to a request by Bishop Brondel for priests and nuns to work among the Northern Cheyenne, four Ursuline Sisters arrived from Toledo, Ohio. A three-room log cabin was built and served as residence, school, dormitory, and even as the church.

The hardships during the years that followed were many. Due to lack of funds, the school was at times on the verge of closing. In 1954, only 64 children were enrolled. As a result of the generosity of many people who had learned of St. Labre, the school survived and began to grow.

In 1965, St. Labre Indian School was asked to extend its support to the Crow Indian Reservation. This resulted in the addition of two campuses—Pretty Eagle Catholic School at St. Xavier and St. Charles Mission School at Pryor.

What we do
St. Labre Indian School at Ashland, Montana. St. Charles Mission School in Pryor, Montana, and Pretty Eagle Catholic School in St. Xavier, Montana. The schools provide elementary and secondary education to Native American students regardless of religious affiliation.

Education is not the only thing that St. Labre provides. St. Labre Youth and Family Services offers counseling to all students and their families. Community outreach is also provided through financial assistance to the Boys and Girls Club of the Northern Cheyenne Nation, Northern Cheyenne Tribal Charities, Crow Tribal Substance Abuse Program, and various Native American cultural celebrations. We see these efforts as a means of strengthening our community. Often, caring for the child means caring for the child's family and environment as well.

In an area where unemployment rates exceed 50%, St. Labre offers the opportunity for productive employment. More than half of our employees are Native American, and we subscribe to a vigorous policy of recruitment from within for job enrichment and advancement. We also strive to recruit from nearby Indian reservations whenever possible.

Another aspect of caring for our community is St. Labre's ongoing effort to curb alcohol and drug abuse. It is impossible to understand the struggle of Native Americans without also understanding the toll taken by alcoholism and drug abuse. It is estimated that every family living on the Indian reservations we serve have been touched by these devastating problems in one form or another. St. Labre provides full-time drug and alcohol counselors to serve our students and their families.

Section V
Support Efforts Focused on specific Illnesses/Issues

55.—THE AMERICAN HEART ASSOCIATION— WWW.AMERICANHEART.ORG

My father died from a heart attack at 75. He kept himself in good shape by walking a lot, lived a good active life and was otherwise in good health until one night when he had a heart attack. He lived a week or ten days, had more attacks and then went into a coma and died. My younger brother died from a heart attack at 60. He just suddenly died one morning just as he was waking up! My sister in law was next to him at the time and his daughter, a nurse, was in the next room. There was nothing they could do. My older brother was visiting relatives in Idaho for a family reunion when he felt bad and was taken to the hodspital. He had total blockage in one artery, was very lucky to have been so close to the hospital where within days he had five-way bypass surgery!

Heart attacks and cardiovascular disease take a whole lot of us—before our time, it seems. The American Heart Association is in the business of doing something about keeping us alive longer.

From the web site:

Please go to the website yourself and peruse the opportunities you fine there—**www.americanheart.org**

56.—CYSTIC FIBROSIS FOUNDATION
WWW.CFF.ORG

The CF Foundation continues to work zealously toward its primary mission of providing a longer and healthier life for those with cystic fibrosis. Over the years much progress has been made and the life expectancy and quality of life for those with CF have improved dramatically. Much headway has been made and there is more to do.

As explained on the web site, the name "65 roses" came from a 4 year old boy who heard his mother calling folks about cyctic Fibrosis and heard it as "65 roses". The name stuck and now the Foundation publishes a calendar full of beautiful pictures of roses each year as a fund raising gift.

From the website: (www.cff.org, Bethesda, MD)
The mission of the Cystic Fibrosis Foundation is to assure the development of the means to cure and control cystic fibrosis and to improve the quality of life for those with the disease.
The Cystic Fibrosis Foundation is proud to be a resource of information about cystic fibrosis. The information provided here should never take the place of advice from your personal health care provider. Be sure to check with your physician about changes in your treatment regimen

Make A Difference In The Lives Of Those With CF!
Cystic fibrosis (CF) is a genetic disease affecting approximately 30,000 children and adults in the United States today. CF causes the body to produce an abnormally thick, sticky mucus, which clogs the airways and leads to life-threatening lung infections. The thick CF mucus also obstructs the pancreas, preventing enzymes from reaching the intestines to help break down and digest food.
The symptoms of CF are diverse, vary in severity, and are often confused with recurrent pneumonia or asthma. The sweat test diagnoses

CF by measuring the amount of salt in the sweat. An abnormally high salt level indicates that a person has CF.

An individual must inherit two defective CF genes—one from each parent—to be born with CF. More than 10 million Americans (one in 31) are symptomless carriers of the defective CF gene.

When the Cystic Fibrosis Foundation was founded in 1955, few children with CF lived to attend elementary school. Today, the median age of survival for an individual with CF extends into the early 30s.

Progress Toward a Cure

The CF Foundation strongly believes that an investment in medical research is an investment in the future of people. When scientists supported by the Foundation discovered the CF gene in 1989, they began a new era in our campaign to defeat this deadly disease.

With the gene identified, they developed the technology to treat the root cause of CF and not just the symptoms. By quickly translating what they learn about the CF gene and CF cells in the laboratory, researchers are developing promising new treatments. The CF Foundation is partnered with several leading companies to ensure that cutting-edge technology is applied to the effort to develop new treatments for CF.

Currently, many clinical trials on new drug treatments are being conducted. These trials will determine the best treatments to improve the length and quality of life for people with CF. Meanwhile, scientists are connecting new clues between defective CF cells, chronic lung infections and a naturally occurring, antibiotic-like substance which malfunctions in CF. Their insights will lead to drugs that target CF lung infections.

Translating basic science discoveries about CF into new treatments will be achieved even faster through the CF Foundation's Therapeutics Development Program. This innovative program includes a specialized network of clinical research centers designed to carry out the early stages of drug development. The program also provides matching grants to biopharmaceutical companies and exciting new technology which will allow researchers to evaluate thousands of potential compounds that could become new drugs to treat CF.

How Dollars Are Spent

The Cystic Fibrosis Foundation puts funds to work as efficiently as possible to support:

- a nationwide network of more than 115 specialty **care centers** dedicated to treating CF;

- a network of **research** and **gene therapy centers** at major universities across the United States;

- **research grants** for top investigators; fellowships for basic and clinical research.

We Need You!

- Please raise awareness in your community about CF and of the strides being made toward a cure.

- Carry the message that specialized care at a CF Foundation-accredited **care center** can contribute to a better quality and longer life for people with CF.

- Access our Web site at **www.cff.org**, or call us at **(800) FIGHT CF**, to learn more about the services and programs available to people with CF.

57.—WOMEN'S STATUS AND THE RISK OF AIDS—NYTIMES FEB. 26, 2001, P. A7— WWW.AMFAR.ORG

"When women have no say in sex, they cannot prevent infection." The article points out how the cultural practices in certain parts of Africa and India are condemning many women to death. More than half of the people infected by AIDS are women in Africa.

From the web site:

amfAR's mission is to prevent HIV infection and the disease and death associated with it and to protect the human rights of all people threatened by the epidemic of HIV/AIDS.

amfAR's Founding: An Interview with Arnold W. Klein, M.D.
Arnold W. Klein was a founding Board member of the Los Angeles-based National AIDS Research Foundation (NARF), which was incorporated in August 1985. (In New York, Mathilde Krim, Ph.D., and others had founded the AIDS Medical Foundation in 1983.) When NARF merged with the American Medical Foundation in September 1985 to form the American Foundation for AIDS Research (amfAR), Dr. Klein was a founding Board member. In addition to maintaining a thriving dermatology practice in Beverly Hills, Dr. Klein continues to serve on amfAR's Board and is active in both Board development and fund-raising efforts. He is also a professor of dermatology/medicine at the University of California, Los Angeles, and a member of the medical staff at Cedars-Sinai Medical Center.

The following article excerpts a recent conversation with Dr. Klein, in which he reflects on his initial involvement with the epidemic, the creation of NARF and amfAR, and what keeps him motivated in the fight against HIV/AIDS.

INITIAL INVOLVEMENT

I first became interested in this just-emerging disease because I diagnosed one of the first cases of HIV-related Kaposi's sarcoma (KS) in Los Angeles, as well as what was then called Gay-Related Immunodeficiency (GRID). This was in around 1981, and I began seeing a lot of patients with recurring infections and that type of thing. It was also around this time that Michael Gottlieb, M.D. [the UCLA scientist who was among the first to report on a new acquired immune deficiency syndrome], published a report on pneumocystis carinii pneumonia (PCP) among young men with suppressed immune systems in the *New England Journal of Medicine.* I was at UCLA then, and Michael and I began discussing his findings on a regular basis. At that time we didn't have any idea what was causing these infections. In fact, it wasn't until the winter of 1985 that we had a blood test for HIV, but in retrospect I saw a lot of prominent people with HIV from very early on in the epidemic.

A lot of things happened together around this time. I was seeing a lot of the early cases, and I was referring many of them to Michael. But most doctors were unaware of what was happening. It became increasingly obvious that we were dealing with a pathogen that was transmitted sexually, but no one was doing anything about it. You had a gay community that began to realize that the party was over, so to speak, and you had a straight community that believed the disease only affected gay people, which wasn't something they cared about particularly. I felt that we needed to do something to address the problem in some way, because I thought that this disease would pose a critical challenge to medicine.

WITHOUT DOCTORS, WITHOUT GOVERNMENT

One of the most disturbing things about these early years is that you could tell we were confronting a disease that would affect vast numbers of people, but people were behaving as if nothing was happening. I was alarmed at the lack of caring I saw. Very few people were advocating safer sex practices. It was just a very strange time…reminiscent of *The Trial* by Franz Kafka.

I thought it was essential that the government get involved in funding research, developing a blood test, that kind of thing. And I knew that no matter how it was transmitted, this was not a disease caused by dance music—it was going to be widespread. It really was like the dawning of a plague, and I had lots and lots of patients coming to me in large part because I was willing to diagnose HIV or AIDS. A lot of doctors weren't willing to deal with the sexuality of their patients. Maybe they had married patients, or patients who were very prominent, or who they didn't want to believe were gay, so doctors helped hide the disease. They ignored it, and ignorance and fear were the biggest problems.

CREATING THE NATIONAL AIDS RESEARCH FOUNDATION (NARF)

The official Board of Directors listed in the NARF incorporation document dated August 13, 1985, were Sheldon W. Andelson, Esq., Michael S. Gottlieb, M.D., Christopher Hersey, Arnold W. Klein, M.D., Charles A. Larson, Esq., William J. Misenhimer, David Sanders, M.D., The Honorable Rand Schrader, Peter Scott, Esq., Michael J. Roth, M.D., Robert Winters, M.D., and Joel D. Weisman, D.O.

I remember coming back from Europe on the Queen Elizabeth II, and I got a cable from Michael that Rock Hudson had been diagnosed with AIDS. By this time Michael and I had begun our ongoing discussions about the disease, and he said that he was going to try to get funding for medical research.

I personally had very little idea of how to set up a medical foundation, but I knew it had to be done. It was just clear that this was a problem that was going to require a great deal of targeted medical research.

The minutes from the August 14, 1985, NARF meeting indicate that a gift of $250,000 from Rock Hudson was received, William Misenhimer was named Executive Director, and Mr. Misenhimer announced that Elizabeth Taylor had volunteered to lead a national fund raising effort.

In 1985, Michael Gottlieb secured some funding from Rock Hudson, and our idea was that we should use this money to set up an organization to deal with the epidemic in much the same way that the AIDS Medical Foundation (AMF) was doing in New York. By this time I had already met Mathilde Krim through Lew Wasserman [president and CEO of MCA and owner of Universal Studios] and his wife Edie. In fact, I had a patient in the 1970s with recurrent herpes outbreaks that I thought might be remedied with topical interferon. Knowing that Dr. Krim was very involved in interferon research, I had contacted her then, and she arranged for me to receive interferon for topical use in my patients.

So I was already in touch with Mathilde, and now there was finally a world-famous celebrity—Elizabeth Taylor—who was willing to speak out about HIV and AIDS.

58.—American Cancer Society—<u>WWW.CANCER.ORG</u>

Certainly most of us know someone who died of cancer, has had cancer or has cancer. It's quite pervasive. My grandmother died of cancer but in those days when someone died at 85 we mostly called it old age. My Uncle died of colon cancer but he was not that old! My first wife died of cancer too. And, I have had skin cancer removed twice. You??

From the web site:

About the American Cancer Society
The American Cancer Society (ACS) is a nationwide, community—based voluntary health organization. Headquartered in Atlanta, Georgia, the ACS has state divisions and more than 3,400 local offices. Learn more about ACS, what we do, and our plans for the future by exploring the areas below.

Who We Are
What We Do
Employment
Meetings and Conferences
Land Adams Award
How You Can Help
News

ACS Mission Statements

ACS Mission

The American Cancer Society is the nationwide community—based voluntary health organization dedicated to eliminating cancer as a major health problem by preventing cancer, saving lives, and diminishing suffering from cancer, through research, education, advocacy, and service.

International Mission

The American Cancer Society's international mission concentrates on capacity building in developing cancer societies and on collaboration with other cancer—related organizations throughout the world in carrying out the strategic directions of the American Cancer Society.

59.—Children's Cancer Research Fund—
www.childrenscancer.org

Did you ever notice how many opportunities there are to donate to cancer research? Breast Cancer research, prostate cancer research, other specific cancer organizations, and this one specifically for children's cancer.

From the web site:

In the Beginning—The Katie Hageboeck Story
In 1978, the Hageboecks were a typical Minnesota family. Their lives were sent into a spiral when Katie was diagnosed with cancer. Norm and Diana looked nationwide for the best possible treatment facility for their daughter and found it in their own backyard at the University of Minnesota. Katie received a bone marrow transplant and follow-up treatment at the University of Minnesota. Katie had a long, tough battle ahead of her. In December 1979, Katie died after a valiant fight. She asked her parents to take the money she had saved for a bicycle and help other kids with cancer. This was the start of Children's Cancer Research Fund (CCRF) as we know it today. Katie's story continues to motivate hundreds of volunteers to help eliminate childhood cancer.
You will find other children's stories on the web site as well. It is particularly tugging on our hearts when children get cancer.

President's Message

I have been involved in Children's Cancer Research Fund for nearly 15 years and have the opportunity to spend time with families and kids suffering from childhood cancers. The stories of their battles with the terrible disease have strengthened my personal resolve to do whatever is in my power to support research in the cure, prevention, and treatment of childhood cancers.

For these kids and their families, the University of Minnesota research supported by Children's Cancer Research Fund provides great hope. The strong track record of success in increasing survival rates and improving treatment outcomes gives patients and their families the belief that their battle can be won.

After 21 years of growth locally, Children's Cancer Research Fund is at a critical point in its evolution. Over the last several years, we have pursued strategies to raise funds nationally to support research at the University of Minnesota. The primary fundraising vehicle outside of the Twin Cities has been direct mail—soliciting donations from individual donors, the great majority of whom have had no connection with Children's Cancer Research Fund until they get our letter in the mail. Our direct mail results have far surpassed our hopes and expectations—more then 200,000 new donors for the organization. With this, we have gained great confidence that our "brand" can be developed nationally and that the strategic goals for annual revenues are within reach.

Now we must prepare our organization, including our Board, our staff, and our volunteer base, to make the changes necessary to become a more nationally recognized fundraising organization. The researchers whom we support at the University of Minnesota are positioned to deliver results with each additional dollar we provide—each day bringing use one step closer to a world free of childhood cancer.

Everyone who plays a role in Children's Cancer Research Fund—volunteers, individual and corporate donors, partners, staff—should feel proud of his or her contributions. This organization is making a real difference in the lives of children and families battling cancer and is worth of our support. On behalf of the kids, their families, and the staff and Board of Directors of Children's Cancer Research Fund, thanks for all that your do!

Rick Collins
President

60.—COSMETIC SAVES A CURE FOR SLEEPING SICKNESS (NEW YORK TIMES, 02/ 09/01, P.A1)
WWW.NYTIMES.COM

Sleeping Sickness? Many Americans, I'm sure, do not even know what sleeping sickness is. I happen to know as I can remember being mortally afraid of tsetse flies when I was young, six to ten or so. As the child of missionary parents I lived where my mom and dad went. In the rainforest jungle country of the Congo River Basin lived not only the Smith family, but thousands of tsetse flies of which some were carriers of sleeping sickness and some were not. After one bit you, you had no way of knowing if you would eventually die from that bite or if it was no worse than a mosquito bite from a non-malaria carrying mosquito. I was afraid of those tsetse flies! You could tell the tsetse from other insects. It was similar to a horse or a house fly in appearance but smaller by half than a horse fly and larger by two or three than a house fly. And, they were sneaky! The tsetse flies would fly around stealthily as if they knew if they came out in the open you would rather smash them than anything.

In the New York Times (02/09/01 p. A1—**www.nytimes.com**) there is an article with the headline shown above, **"Cosmetic Saves a Cure for Sleeping Sickness."**
The article, by Donald McNeil, Jr., explains what is currently going on with certain drug companies that make a substance that is known to cure sleeping sickness (human African trypanosomiasis). It seems the drug companies have not made much of the drug (eflornithine) as hopes that it would fight cancer have not panned out. The 300,000 Africans in war-torn central Africa do not have the money to pay for the drug.

Recently it was discovered that the drug is effective in removing facial hair and it is now being produced and advertised for that purpose. Since they are making a lot of money from the sale of the hair control product, Doctors Without Borders (see number 41) is working with the drug companies to guarantee a low cost supply of the drug for the indefinite future. Yea for Doctors Without Borders! Could you support them? Could you do something to encourage the Drug Companies to participate in the less affluent parts of our planet and get diseases like sleeping sickness under control when we can?

61.—NATIONAL FEDERATION OF THE BLIND—<u>WWW.NFB.ORG</u>

While I was employed at Lucent Technologies I had the opportunity to interact with a few blind people as Lucent had a policy of hiring people with disabilities when they could do the work and assisting them as needed. For example, I got to read feedback data to a couple of the blind employees when we had a peer feedback process with results printed by computer but not in Braille. After getting to know them a little I would say "Hi" when I saw them in the hall. I noticed that it would be up to me to say "hi" first as they didn't know me well enough to recognize who I was by my footsteps! And, it would probably be useful for me to say who I was, at least until it was clear they recognized the sound of my voice.

The National Federation of the Blind has these recommendations:

- Take time to learn what blind people are really like. Get to know one of us on a personal basis. First hand knowledge make a difference.

- Promote Braille literacy. Insist that blind children be taught Braille in the public schools. Blind children who can't read, can't compete. Urgent action is needed.

- Tell an employer that blind people can be good employees. Blind people face a 74% unemployment rate. You can help.

- Recruit volunteers interested in reading or driving for blind persons, or assisting with shopping needs.

- Urge anyone you know who is losing eyesight to seek help. Seventy-five thousand people in the United States become blind each year. Most know almost nothing about the capabilities of blind people or the help that exists. Prompt action can prevent needless despair and suffering.

The National Federation of the Blind
1800 Johnson Street
Baltimore, MD 21230-4998

If you or someone you know needs assistance with problems of blindness, please write or call:

Patricia A. Maurer
Director of Community Relations
National Federation of the Blind
1800 Johnson Street
Baltimore, MD 21230-4998
communityrelations@nfb.org
(410) 659-9314, ext. 272

From the web site:

About the NFB

Founded in 1940, the National Federation of the Blind (NFB) is the nation's largest and most influential membership organization of **blind** persons. With fifty thousand members, the NFB has **affiliates** in all fifty states plus Washington D.C. and Puerto Rico, and over seven hundred local chapters. As a consumer and advocacy organization, the NFB is considered the leading force in the blindness field today.

The purpose of the National Federation of the Blind is two-fold—to help blind persons achieve self-confidence and self-respect and to act as a vehicle for collective self-expression by the blind. By providing public education about blindness, information and referral services, **scholarships**, **literature** and publications about blindness, **aids and appliances** and other adaptive equipment for the blind, advocacy services and protection of civil rights, development and evaluation of

technology, and support for blind persons and their families, members of the NFB strive to educate the public that the blind are normal individuals who can compete on terms of equality.

Special services of the National Federation of the Blind include a Materials Center containing over eleven hundred pieces of literature about blindness and four hundred different aids and appliances used by the blind and the **International Braille and Technology Center** for the Blind is the world's largest and most complete evaluation and demonstration center for all speech and Braille technology used by the blind from around the world. **NFB-NEWSLINE**® for the Blind, the world's first free talking newspaper service, offers the blind the complete text of leading national and local newspapers with the use of only a touch-tone telephone. **Jobline**® offers national employment listings and job openings through a telephone menu system to anyone free of charge.

Publications of the NFB include the ***Braille Monitor***, which provides a positive philosophy about blindness and discusses events and activities of the Federation and in the blindness field and
Future Reflections, a publication of the National Organization of Parents of Blind Children, a Division of the NFB. ***Voice of the Diabetic*** focuses on special interests and needs of diabetics and is a publication of the Diabetes Action Network, also a Division of the National Federation of the Blind.

It is estimated that about 1.1 million people in the U.S. are blind. Each year 50,000 more will become blind. Studies show that only AIDS and cancer are feared more than blindness. However, blindness need not be the tragedy which it is generally thought to be. In the NFB we say, "The real problem of blindness is not the loss of eyesight, but the misunderstanding and lack of information which exist."

62.—GUIDE DOGS FOR THE BLIND
WWW.GUIDEDOG.ORG

I heard on the radio one day, a person talking about how they train guide dogs for the blind. The thing that struck me was when they said they "only use positive feedback" during the training process. No smacking on the nose when the dog doesn't do it right!

I have quoted this often. I say, "If it is good enough for dogs, it ought to be good enough for human beings!"

From the web site:

Since 1946, the Guide Dog Foundation for the Blind, Inc. has provided guide dogs free of charge to blind people who seek enhanced mobility and independence.

Our students come to us from all over the United States and many foreign countries. Our trademark small classes and individualized instruction often attract students who may have special requirements. We have successfully trained hearing-impaired blind people as well as many physically challenged people.

We are supported entirely by donations from generous individuals, corporations and foundations. We receive no government funding.

The Guide Dog Foundation is proud of its reputation as a charitable organization. The Foundation consistently has received high marks from charitable watchdog organizations. To learn more about how the Guide Dog Foundation rates with these groups, visit our listings on these Web sites:

- **The American Institute of Philanthropy**

- **GuideStar—The Donor's Guide To The Charitable Universe**

- **<u>Better Business Bureau Wise Giving Alliance</u>**

63.—HELPING THE BLIND IN INDIA—

A fellow employee of Lucent Technologies (when I used to work there before retiring in 2000) was one of the five people who started a fund-raising effort to assist blind people in India (his country of origin) regain their sight when possible. If you take a look at the web site you'll see that they have raised hundreds of thousands of dollars for the cause they espoused. A few dedicated individuals can in deed create a sizable contribution!

From the web site: (no longer available)

Five Lucent employees have established the Blind Foundation for India. The organization's mission is to prevent blindness in India, and cure it when possible. The foundation is not affiliated with the Lucent Technologies Foundation.

Blind Foundation for India was founded in 1989 by a team headed by Dr. Manu Vora, Voice of The Customer manager for Lucent Technologies customer technical support organization in Naperville, Ill.

Staggering Statistics:

- One out of every three blind people in the world lives in India—an estimated **13 million blind** people live in India.

- Every year, **2.3 million** people **develop cataracts** in their eyes.

- There are **2 million blind children** in India. Only 5% of them receive any education.

64.—RECORDING FOR THE BLIND & DYSLEXIC, RFB&D® WWW.RFBD.ORG

At **www.rfbd.org** you will find out about recording for the blind and dyslexic. Donations fund the activities or you could become one of the over 5,000 volunteers who do the reading at the over 30 studios.

From the organization and from the web site:

For more than 50 years, Recording for the Blind & Dyslexic, a non-profit volunteer organization, has been the nation's educational library serving people who cannot effectively read standard print because of visual impairment, dyslexia, or other physical disability. Our mission is to create opportunities for individual success by providing, and promoting the effective use of, accessible educational materials. In addition to developing state-of-the-art reading technologies that make educational materials more accessible to students with disabilities, RFB&D has also expanded its mission to offer effective strategies to help maximize the benefits of auditory learning. For more information, please call toll free 866-RFBD-585 or visit our award-winning accessible website at **www.rfbd.org**.

Our recording technologies have changed with the times. Sound-Scriber discs were long ago replaced with the high-fidelity, four-track cassettes still in use today. Soon, digital audio technology will be introduced to our members, allowing them access to the more than 93,000 titles in our CV Starr Learning Through Listening™ Master Library on CD.

RFB&D now has a volunteer force of more than 5,200 volunteers who added 4,011 titles to our library in the year 2002. RFB&D has also undertaken an innovative educational outreach initiative—bringing our services directly into the schools to train teachers and students how to most effectively use our services.

As an example of what is on the web site, in my hometown I found the following: *Naperville Studio* 30 No. Brainard Street, Naperville, IL 60540 Billie Mater, Studio Director, 630-420-0722 Located on the campus of North Central College, the Naperville Studio is in need of daytime volunteers to assist in the recording and editing of math and science textbooks for blind and dyslexic students. We offer comprehensive training and flexible scheduling. After training is completed, a person can volunteer any weekday between 7 a.m. and 10 p.m. This studio has since moved to: 1266 East Chicago Avenue
Naperville, IL 60540
Phone: (630) 420-0722

You can make a difference.

Well, I did contact the Naperville studio. I went to visit one snowy day in the winter of 2000-2001. The studio was tucked away on the fourth floor of a building on the local college campus. I thought I would get trained and give some of my time to recording for the blind. I went twice for training and then the studio was shut down for a month or so while they moved to new, expanded, quarters in a strip mall not far away. I never went back. I had thoughts about it, and found myself completely busy with other things and the initial excitement had worn off. It turns out I wasn't committed to that as an activity for my time—maybe later? The people I met were quite dedicated to doing the recording and were quite nice. Maybe it was the reading of mathematical formulas that didn't excite me—not all the reading, of course, is mathematics texts. It just happened the session at which I was being trained was a math book. Maybe I did enough of that in school?

65.—ORBIS FLYING-FOR-SIGHT CLUB—WWW.ORBIS.ORG

When the ORBIS request for a donation came to my mailbox I thought "this is a rather unique approach". Put a hospital in an airplane and fly to where the eye surgeries are needed! Seems this has been going on now for almost 20 years. Each person finds their own way to contribute to their fellow man (woman).

From the web site:

Profile:
ORBIS—An Introduction
ORBIS envisions a world in which avoidable blindness is eliminated. A world of quality eye care and treatment for every human being, especially for the more than 180 million who are blind, severely visually impaired or at risk of becoming blind. Right now, 80 percent of those who are blind do not need to be. Millions can be cured with techniques routinely practiced in many countries.

A global humanitarian organization, ORBIS works in developing countries to save sight through hands-on training, public health education, and improved access to eye care. Since 1982, ORBIS has completed more than 440 programs in 80 countries. It has trained in excess of 50,000 ophthalmologists, nurses, biomedical engineers and other health care workers who, in turn, provide treatment and training in their countries. Worldwide, more than 23,070 patients have been directly treated by ORBIS volunteer doctors and more than nine million people have received eye care from ORBIS-trained doctors.

ORBIS has developed an ambitious strategic plan outlining its efforts to eliminate avoidable blindness. The plan utilizes three program models: Comprehensive, multi-year country programs; short-term country programs tailored to the need of partnering institutions and the regions they serve; and training programs in ophthalmic subspecialties with or without the ORBIS DC-10 flying eye hospital. The foundation of the ORBIS program is the DC-10 flying eye surgery hospital and teaching facility. A converted jet aircraft, the ORBIS DC-10 travels to developing countries where the 25-member ORBIS international medical team and visiting volunteer doctors perform eye surgeries—sharing their skills with eye care professionals from the host nation.

ORBIS also conducts surgical, nursing, biomedical engineering, and system support training at local hospitals.

Many Ambassadors, Heads of State, Ministers of Health and other government officials around the world have expressed their admiration and support for ORBIS's programs and its active diplomatic role.

Funds for the US$25 million annual budget come from a variety sources including gifts, grants and gifts-in-kind from major corporations, foundations, government agencies and individuals around the world.

WHAT ORBIS DOES TO ERADICATE WORLD-BLINDNESS

According to the World Health Organization (WHO), more than 45 million people in the world are blind and an additional 135 million people have low vision and are at great risk of becoming blind. The knowledge and technology to reverse or prevent 80 percent of worldwide blindness already exists. However, nine in ten of those suffering from blindness live in developing countries where doctors lack the necessary training and equipment to restore sight.

Understanding the urgent need for continuing medical education, ORBIS converted a DC-8 and then a DC-10 jet aircraft into a flying eye-hospital and teaching center. The aircraft flies to developing countries, bringing crucial surgical and technical training to local eye doctors, nurses, and health care personnel. Training is conducted by volunteer ophthalmologists selected from a worldwide network of over 375 doctors. The doctors work with ORBIS in the field for one week at a time, sharing their knowledge and experience with host-country doctors.

Each week during comprehensive plane missions, ORBIS doctors work with the local host committee to select a range of patients whose treatable eye conditions provide excellent cases for demonstrating modern techniques and procedures. Lectures and surgery are conducted during the middle of the week along with post-operative care.

The ORBIS strategy of training trainers lowers program costs while extending the reach and impact of programs. ORBIS works with host-country medical leaders to identify potential participants who have the capacity to serve as trainers for their colleagues once the program is finished. Participants selected receive one-on-one, hands-on-training from visiting faculty while others observe the procedures from the classroom.

The ORBIS plane also attracts media and government attention wherever it goes. This high-level exposure enables ORBIS to serve as a catalyst for nationwide solutions to the problem of blindness, such as the establishment of eye banks and the creation of national plans for the prevention of blindness.

THE NEED CONTINUES

The World Health Organization reports that the aging of the world's population, combined with the population growth in developing countries, will mean a doubling of the number of blind people in the world by the year 2020. During the next 25 years, the number of blind could climb as high as 80 million with more than 200 million others at risk, a pace far faster than the predicted rate of overall population growth.

Today, 20 million people cannot see, or see poorly, simply because of cataracts. Others are blind because of corneal opacities, glaucoma, or retinal problems. In most cases, a cure or treatment for these common conditions is available.

Less widespread eye conditions such as trachoma in desert countries, river blindness in tropical areas, and childhood blindness related to Vitamin A deficiency can be treated through drug therapy. Medical research has produced low-cost drugs or treatments to cure or arrest these conditions.

Unfortunately, these important advances rarely reach much of the developing world. The only sustainable solution to the problem of needless blindness is to provide the medical community in developing countries with the skills, knowledge and resources necessary to prevent and cure blindness.

With on-going support, health care workers in developing countries can use improved skills and modern equipment to help eradicate the tragedy of avoidable blindness. Continued support of ORBIS programs will help millions of people retain or regain their vision because more and more doctors will have the requisite knowledge to prevent and treat blindness.

Section VI
Support Efforts Focused on American Veterans

66.—PARALYZED VETERANS OF AMERICA—<u>WWW.PVA.ORG</u>

Here is one of several Veterans organization that seems worthy of support. I have a friend who is a Vietnam Veteran. I asked him once "What was the hardest thing about being a Vietnam Vet.?" He said, "Being spit on when I came back from the war." Let's support our Veterans no matter what!

Mission Statement
The Paralyzed Veterans of America, a congressionally chartered veterans service organization founded in 1946, has developed a unique expertise on a wide variety of issues involving the special needs of our members-veterans of the armed forces who have experienced spinal cord injury or dysfunction.
PVA will use that expertise to be the leading advocate for:

• Quality health care for our members,

• Research and education addressing spinal cord injury and dysfunction,

• Benefits available as a result of our members' military service,

• Civil rights and opportunities which maximize the independence of our members.

To enable PVA to continue to honor this commitment, we must recruit and retain members who have the experience, energy, dedication, and passion necessary to manage the organization and ensure adequate resources to sustain the programs essential for PVA to achieve its mission.

67.—HELP HOSPITALIZED VETERANS—WWW.HHV.ORG

Here is yet another organization to provide assistance to our veterans. Help them out!

From the web site:

HHV celebrates 30 Years Of Service to Disabled, Sick and Wounded Veterans!

Hospitalized veterans, staff, donors and HHV personnel were recently treated to parties celebrating HHV's 30 years of service to our veterans. Hosting these parties were the Tampa Bay and Bay Pines VA Hospitals. 30 years of service to America's hospitalized veterans is really something to celebrate!

The hospitalized veterans told everyone just what HHV does to enrich their lives on a daily basis. They couldn't say enough about what part the Craft Kits have played in their lives and about the loyal and dedicated donors.

Several of the donors who attended spoke about how this program has affected their lives. In addition to donations of funds for Craft Kits, they told about donations of their time as volunteers in the hospitals.

The hospital staff said that they couldn't get along without the Craft Kits. They are vital to the recovery of many patients. The Kits are often part of the patient's prescription for recovery.

68.—AMVETS NATIONAL SERVICE FOUNDATION— WWW.AMVETS.ORG

For a few years the local AMVETS were the recipients of all our household donations of clothing, books, and other household items that we were no longer needing. Every two months or so when a pile of things had accumulated, I would drive a few bags and boxes of "stuff" to the place where AMVETS had a truck trailer. There was a veteran to load it and give me a receipt for income tax purposes. Recently GOODWILL, another organization that collects used goods to recycle built a very convenient drop off place for our donations and so I have switched from AMVETS to GOODWILL for our donations. That doesn't mean I don't continue to support AMVETS. I think they do good work!

From the web site:

Serving America's Veterans…
…with Pride…
…with Honor…
…with Commitment

The above phrases are not just words ~ they are what we believe and what we do—they define what being an *AMVETS* member means. From the halls of Congress, where we advocate legislation of benefit to all Veterans, to the streets of America, where we may be working to get a homeless Vet a warm and safe place to sleep, we strive to ensure that *AMVETS* represents the very best that America has to offer.

In short, we are YOU ~ Veterans associated with each other who realize that when we were mustered out, our service and our commitment to our nation did not end, it just entered a new phase. We consider ALL Veterans to be our comrades. We make no distinction among the

Armed Services, no distinction between genders, no distinction based upon race, religion, or political affiliation.

WE ARE AMERICAN VETERANS
Serving
AMERICA'S VETERANS

69.—DISABLED AMERICAN VETERANS—WWW.DAV.ORG

I was 10 years old when WWII ended. Old enough to have a vague idea of what it might be like to be in the trenches being shot at and shooting at others...looking death in the face. I knew it was a good cause the USA fought for and had I been older I would have been in it. However, I've also been relieved that I never had to make that choice. The visceral feelings I had when thinking about being a soldier have always given me a deep appreciation for those who gave their lives, those who were injured and disabled, and those who faced those possibilities and survived relatively unscathed. That has made giving to the Disabled American Veterans an obvious and easy contribution to make.

From the web site:

Background Information on the Disabled American Veterans
Treaties are signed and the battles of nations end, but the personal battles of those disabled in war only begin when the guns fall silent. These men and women must struggle to regain health, reshape lives shattered by disability, learn new trades or professions, and rejoin the civilian world. At each step, they need help to help themselves. For three quarters of a century now, that aid has come from the Disabled American Veterans (DAV), a nonprofit organization of more than one million veterans disabled during time of war or armed conflict.
Formed in 1920 and chartered by Congress in 1932, the million-member DAV is the official voice of America's service-connected disabled veterans—a strong, insistent voice that represents all of America's 2.1 million disabled veterans, their families and survivors. Its nationwide network of services—free of charge to all veterans and members of their families—is totally supported by membership dues and contribu-

tions from the American public. Not a government agency, the DAV's national organization receives no government funds.

Section VII
Ideas to consider and/or support

70.—Trade not Aid (see TIME 10/23/00)
WWW.TIME.COM

"Trade not Aid" is Bringing Entrepreneurs together in Developing Countries.

From the web site:

In a *TIME Magazine* (10/23/00) **www.time.com**, an article by Helena Bachmann covers a story about David Dichter who is matching up entrepreneurs from developing countries and helping them form profitable alliances. His company, Technology for the People, was founded in 1977 and based in Geneva Switzerland. A key to the successes he brokers is the use of technology appropriate to the local economies of the countries involved. In countries where the economy doesn't include large amounts of capital, equipment or technical know-how is used as equity in a way that is satisfactory to both partners. For example, he recently brokered a joint venture between an Indian Company and a company in Georgia (formerly part of the USSR) to manufacture solar hot-water heating systems for sale in Georgia. The production technology and marketing savvy come from India and the raw materials and factory and office facilities come from the company in Georgia. No capital was involved.

71.—APPRECIATIVE INQUIRY—SEE HTTP:// APPRECIATIVEINQUIRY.CWRU.EDU/INTRO/ CONFERENCE.CFM FOR OCTOBER 3, 2001 CONFERENCE

"Appreciative Inquiry (AI) is a powerful vehicle for accelerating change.
Through collaborative inquiry and strategic visioning, organizations, teams, and individuals unleash the human energy and imagination necessary to spark powerful innovations and radically transform their future." This statement is from a brochure inviting people to attend The First International Conference on Appreciative Inquiry
That is scheduled for September 30—October 3, 2001 in Baltimore Maryland.

From the web site:

First International Appreciative Inquiry Conference
Baltimore, Maryland
September 30—October 2, 2001

The First International Conference on Appreciative Inquiry opened just three weeks after the terrorist attacks on the World Trade Center in New York City and the US Pentagon. After the attacks, the conference design team met to decide whether to proceed with the conference. After much soul searching, we decided that if ever there was a time when the world needed to develop affirmative competence, it is now. However, we decided to refine the design to place the focus on how business might serve as an agent of world benefit.

Another last minute addition was the possible connection of the AI conference with a conference scheduled for New York City for April 21—23 that would focus on Spirit in Business. This conference would feature His Holiness the Dalai Lama and the opening evening would be co-hosted by Dave Cooperrider and Peter Senge. It was determined that we would include the possibility of linking to this spring conference in the work we did at the AI conference and more important that we would recast the conference to address what felt like a pressing question, "what would it be like if business were an agent of world benefit?"

For reasons we can only imagine, the total number of registrants for this conference not only didn't drop, it increased between September 11 and the conference, which opened on September 30th. Over 500 people attended the conference. In spite of nervousness around the world about travel, people arrived from Europe, the Middle East, Africa, Asia, Australia and New Zealand, and South America. At 5 PM on Sunday Jane Watkins opened the conference welcoming everyone on behalf of the conference hosts: Appreciative Inquiry Consulting, Benedictine University, National Training Labs, and the Weatherhead School of Management at Case Western Reserve University. She suggested that we were about to engage in a conversation and that would co-create it together. She then introduced Dave Cooperrider and Diana Whitney who began the first plenary session, which was about the Discovery Phase of Appreciative Inquiry.

72.—"SAUDI TO DIRECT UN PROGRAM AIMED AT CONTROLLING POPULATION"—UNITED NATIONS POPULATION FUND WWW.NYTIMES.COM

This was a headline on Page A5 of the *New York Times* INTERNATIONAL on October 26, 2000. The short story was about the appointment of Thoraya Ahmed Obaid, an American-educated woman, to executive director of the United Nations Population Fund. This activity has made the expansion of women's rights central to its mission of cutting population growth worldwide. She replaces Nafis Sadik of Pakistan, who retires later in 2000 after presiding over a revolutionary decade in thinking about population at the United Nations, which has moved from basic family planning programs into broad areas of reproductive health and freedom of choice.
We wish her well!!

See also number 84 another **www.nytimes.com** article about this same woman.

73.—A GLOBAL TREATY TO CURB TOBACCO USE!
WWW.WHO.INT/HOME-PAGE/

New York Times INTERNATIONAL—10/22/2000 p. 4.

As an ex-smoker this headline caught my eye. I smoked for thirty years up until about 18 years ago. When people ask me how long it took me to quit I say "30 years!". Since I never really wanted to smoke, I was thinking about quitting throughout my 30 year smoking career. Finally, I got to see that I could be in charge of my life and not those tobacco sticks!

So, I am highly in favor of curbing (read eliminating) the use of tobacco for smoking. I'm rather obnoxious about smokers at times—believe it or not.

So, this article was about officials from nearly 150 countries, in an atmosphere of unexpected harmony, laying the groundwork for a new global treaty that aims to control tobacco use and stamp out adolescent smoking.

The World Health Organization (WHO) is pushing for a strong international accord with the goal of finalizing a treaty by 2003. The United Nations agency, the WHO, has made eradicating smoking the centerpiece of its global public health strategy and wants the treaty to ban multinational tobacco corporations from advertising and sponsoring sports events, increase taxes to make cigarettes more expensive, combat cigarette smuggling and introduce measures to stem the rise in adolescent smoking.

We wish this effort well indeed. I can't stand to be in the presence of smokers now—even though I used to be a chimney!

Try the following website for more information about the World Health Organization.

http://www.who.int/home-page/

74.—THE INTERNATIONAL CONFERENCE ON BUSINESS AND CONSCIOUSNESS— WWW.BIZSPIRIT.COM

This international conference will be held for the eighth time in Santa Fe NM, January, 2003. See: **www.bizspirit.com**

From the web site:

Once in a while,
something comes along
that marks a moment we remember
as having forever changed our life…
…a door opens, we walk through and when we turn and look back for that same opening, it no longer exists. We become different.
Many participants have told us that this conference has been that door, through which there is no return. They said they were changed, and were amazed at what happened when they found themselves among others to whom business with consciousness is essential.
"Why didn't you tell us in your brochure about the power of this conference?" one asked. We thought-*"It's hard to capture in words, the essence of something like this. How do you describe an awakening to someone else unless they've experienced it for themselves?"* So we won't attempt to tell you, but rather invite you to <u>read the words of others like you.</u> And then come and find out for yourself.

Reflecting the increasing interest in Integrity, Authenticity, Balance, Sustainability, Purpose, Creativity, Leadership and Greatness—along with Profit at work—the International Conference on Business and Consciousness is one of the few conferences that grew in 2002—enjoying a 26% increase in attendance from the previous year.

75.—THE DALAI LAMA SAYS…AND
WWW.SAVETIBET.ORG

This guy just might be worth listening to?
The Dalai Lama was awarded the Nobel Peace prize in 1989.

From the web site:

The **International Campaign for Tibet** (ICT) works to promote human rights and self-determination for Tibetans and to protect their culture and environment. ICT has offices in Washington, D.C., and Amsterdam.

The Dalai Lama's Message on the Anniversary of September 11 (1-Sep)
The Dalai Lama has called for long-term preventative measures to oppose terrorism, saying that these would be more effective than taking violent steps. In a message to commemorate the first anniversary of the September 11 tragedy, the Dalai Lama said that he understood the temptation to respond with violence but felt that a cautious approach would be more fruitful.

From my email:

An email has been being passed around with the following message: (I'm not promoting the "spamming" that this could be. I am promoting the idea that these ideas are worth looking at!) This is what The Dalai Lama has to say on the millennium. All it takes is a few seconds to read and think over. *(Do not keep this message. The mantra must leave your hands within 96 hours. You will get a very pleasant surprise. This is true even if you are not superstitious.)* It's up to you if you want to share this.

INSTRUCTIONS FOR LIFE

1. Take into account that great love and great achievements involve great risk.

2. When you lose, don't lose the lesson.

3. Follow the three Rs: Respect for self Respect for others and Responsibility for all your actions.

4. Remember that not getting what you want is sometimes a wonderful stroke of luck.

5. Learn the rules so you know how to break them properly.

6. Don't let a little dispute injure a great friendship.

7. When you realize you've made a mistake, take immediate steps to correct it.

8. Spend some time alone every day.

9. Open your arms to change, but don't let go of your values.

10. Remember that silence is sometimes the best answer.

11. Live a good, honorable life. Then when you get older and think back, you'll be able to enjoy it a second time.

12. A loving atmosphere in your home is the foundation for your life.

13. In disagreements with loved ones, deal only with the current situation. Don't bring up the past.

14. Share your knowledge. It's a way to achieve immortality.

15. Be gentle with the earth.

6. Once a year, go someplace you've never been before.

17. Remember that the best relationship is one in which your love for each other exceeds your need for each other.

18. Judge your success by what you had to give up in order to get it.

19. Approach love and cooking with reckless abandon.

FORWARD THIS MANTRA E-MAIL TO AT LEAST 5 PEOPLE AND YOUR LIFE WILL IMPROVE. (That's up to you.)

76.—A World That Works
www.aworldthatworks.com

At this web site you will find a list of 18 SOLVABLE global issues. Number one on the list is "Eliminating Starvation/Feeding Humanity". Let's get to work!

From the web site:

Try speaking these declarations out loud, perhaps in unison, at your next gathering.

DECLARATIONS FOR A WORLD THAT WORKS FOR EVERYONE
www.AWorldThatWorks.com
TODAY AND FOR ALL TIME,
The world works for every person on the planet.

TODAY AND FOR ALL TIME,
Every child and parent is loved, taken care of, supported, and nurtured for their entire lives.
The world is living in peace.
Every human being on the planet has enough to eat and be nurtured.
Everyone has access to medical care and attention.

TODAY AND FOR ALL TIME,
Every human being has a safe home.
Every person has plenty of clean water to drink.
Every person knows how to read and finds joy in learning.
The earth is using all energy effectively and imaginatively.

TODAY AND FOR ALL TIME,
There is plenty of energy available for everyone.
Every country is debt free and prosperous.

The world's population is stable and perfectly aligned with its resources.

Crops are thriving and soil is stable throughout the world.

TODAY AND FOR ALL TIME,

The world's forests are thriving and regenerating.

The ozone layer is healthy and protected.

Our worldwide air and skies are clean.

The temperatures of the planet are stable and perfect.

TODAY AND FOR ALL TIME,

The earth is clear of all land mines.

Every citizen of the world belongs to a community where they are valued.

Weapons of mass destruction and radioactive waste have been permanently disposed of.

Every person lives in freedom with respect for speech and law.

Copyright by Robert Adler, 2001. www.AWorldThatWorks.com

Useful Links

Below are some links to websites of organizations whose missions and/ or interests are similar to ours. On the **Major World Issues** page, you can find links to other websites containing useful information about the 20 global issues we are concerned with on this website.

- **Buckminster Fuller Institute**

- **Co-op America**

- **The Fourth Wave: A Normative Forecast for the Future of SpaceShip Earth**

- **Global Energy Network Institute (GENI)**

- **Interdisciplinary Studies: Global Issues in Society**

- **<u>Landmark Education Corporation</u>**

- **<u>Peace Room: The Foundation for Conscious Evolution</u>**

- **<u>Planet Project</u>**

- **<u>State of the World Forum</u>**

- **<u>United Nations</u>**

- **<u>Utopia & Utopian Philosophy</u>**

- **<u>Which World: Scenarios for the 21st Century</u>**

- **<u>World Game Institute</u>**

- **<u>World Game Institute Index of Global Topics</u>**

- **<u>World Game Institute: What The World Wants Project</u>**

- **<u>World Overpopulation Awareness</u>**

- **<u>World Problems and Global Issues Project</u>**

- **<u>Worldwatch Institute</u>**

77.—JESSE HELMS URGES FOREIGN AID BE HANDLED BY CHARITIES (NOT GOVERNMENTS)
WWW.USAID.GOV

This was the headline for an article I saw in the "New York Times" on January 12th, 2001. It was on page A4. Senator Helms, (previously?) the most powerful critic of foreign aid in Congress, said he would champion an increase in international assistance—but only if all future United States aid was funneled to the needy through private charities and religious groups instead of a government agency. This could mean the end of the Agency for International Development that employs 7,300 people and oversees a $7 billion a year in economic and humanitarian aid budget. The activity would shift to a quasi-governmental foundation that would deliver grants to private and community relief groups. If this proposal is adopted by Congress, it will be the most decisive shift in 40 years in how America a helps the world's downtrodden. Hmmmmm. Might this be a better approach?

The senate web site—**http://www.senate.gov/legislative/index.html**

And Senator Helms' web site—**http://www.senate.gov/~helms/** (as of 2003, Jesse Helms is no longer in the Senate)

From the web site:

Senator Helms began his first term in the Senate in January 1973; was reelected to a second term on November 7, 1978; to a third term on November 6, 1984; a fourth term on November 6, 1990; and a fifth term on November 7, 1996. He is Ranking Minority member of the **Committee on Foreign Relations**, a member of the **Committee on Agriculture, Nutrition and Forestry**, and a member of the **Rules And Administration Committee**.

Now (9/2002) I just looked up **www.usaid.gov** to see if Jesse Helms' proposal in the above article has had an influence over the intervening year. I think it has!

From that web site:

Washington File

18 September 2002
By Kathryn McConnell
Washington File Staff Writer

Washington—The U.S. Agency for International Development (USAID) is spending approximately $130 million on 75 regional and country-specific development alliances less than one year after initiating its Global Development Alliance (GDA) program, a USAID official says.

Briefing reporters and representatives from nongovernmental organizations (NGOs) September 18 in Washington, Holly Wise, director of the GDA program, said the GDA model responds to changes in the development assistance environment Official development assistance is now just 14 percent of total U.S. funding flows to the developing world and funding from private sources is increasing, Wise said.

USAID wants to "turn up the volume on effective partnering" and look for new development alliances among corporations, foundations, universities, NGOs and private voluntary organizations (PVOs), Wise said. She added that alliances could also help leverage the 25 percent of flows to developing countries that are in the form of personal and institutional remittances by reducing transaction costs.

Wise said the new business model has involved organizational change within USAID so that the agency can involve partners and potential partners "at an early stage" to discuss new development ideas. Collaboration between USAID and private partners involves collectively defining and solving specific problems, she said.

Wise said GDA has become central to USAID's planning and programming. Alliances are formed in areas such as basic education, vocational training, information technology, forestry, water, plant gene banks and small enterprise development, she said.

Other international organizations—such as the World Bank and the U.N. Development Program (UNDP)—are also becoming involved in development partnerships, Wise said.

Wise said that USAID works only with partners that are "socially responsible," particularly in the areas of human rights, financial soundness, labor conditions, environmental accountability and affirmative action standards.

She said business partners bring to developing countries such strengths as more foreign direct investment (FDI), experience with leading business practices—especially those related to environmental and workers' issues—and the ability to use buying power to affect change.

Wise pointed to two of USAID's alliances as examples of effective partnering:

1. The Sustainable Forest Products Alliance (SFPA) leverages $6.5 million in USAID funding with $12 million in funding from private sources—including Ikea and Home Depot—to develop and apply responsible forestry principles. The Certified Forest Product Council and World Wildlife Fund are also involved in the alliance.

2. The USAID/Peru Economic Service Centers Alliance leverages $140,000 of USAID/Peru's funding with $1.1 million in funding from Buenaventura Mining Company to operate 10 economic service centers for local entrepreneurs as part of the country's poverty-reduction program.

78.—GREATERGOOD.COM—
WWW.GREATERGOOD.COM

The first I heard of this web site was from an email from someone—I've now forgotten who—who recommended that I click on thehungersite.com every day. I clicked into the site and there I found advertisers willing to pay for us to click in the anticipation that we would also click on their ad and go to a web site to buy something. It must be working as the site continues to operate and now I'm clicking on thehungersite and thebreastcancersite almost every day. As I review this item in the process of revising this book—I'm jumping out to click on thehungersite and thebreastcancersite right now (9/23/02)!

From the web site:

About Us

GreaterGood.com is dedicated to making it free and easy to support good causes through everyday Internet use. Visitors do what they already do online—shop, click, search, sign up for an ISP service, make travel arrangements, apply for a credit card and more—with each action automatically generating revenue for a cause they select at no extra cost to them. People are busy, but they do care about the world they live in. At GreaterGood.com we make it easy and convenient for them to regularly make a tangible difference. In 2000, we generated millions of dollars for organizations such as Special Olympics, Save The Children, The Nature Conservancy, the Muscular Dystrophy Association and over 3000 more.

GreaterGood.com is part of a family of cause-related Web sites operated by CharityUSA.com, LLC, including the world's leading click-to-give sites, The Hunger Site, The Breast Cancer Site, The Rainforest Site and EcologyFund.com.

At the GreaterGood.com shopping portal **(www.greatergood.com)** Internet users can shop at over 100 leading online merchants—including Amazon.com, priceline, Nordstrom, Lands' End, Dell, Office Max, 1-800 flowers and more—and up to 15% of each purchase automatically goes to an organization they select at no extra cost to them. Shoppers can support local and national charities, the nation's K-12 schools and college and university scholarship funds. In 1999, the revenue generated from the GreaterGood.com shopping portal supported many critical activities, including:

- Training 275 Special Olympic athletes

- Financing the Save The Children office in Tuzla, Bosnia

- Upgrading computer equipment in K-12 schools

- Immunizing over 220 children worldwide against six life-threatening diseases

- Saving animals from abandonment and hunger by subsidizing three new spay and neuter clinics

- Funding financial aid and scholarship endowments at national colleges

The Hunger Site **(www.thehungersite.com)** is the world's first "click-to-give" site, where more than 150 million visitors have given more than 250 million cups of free food to help feed the hungry. This is done by visiting The Hunger Site daily and simply clicking the "donate free food" button. The contributions of staple food, paid for by The Hunger Site's sponsors, are distributed to the world's hunger hot-spots by leading hunger relief organizations—Mercy Corps and America's Second Harvest.

In 2000, The Hunger Site has been recognized as an international favorite, winning The People's Voice Award in the Activism category at the fourth annual Webby Awards, the "Oscars of the Internet."

The Breast Cancer Site was founded to help offer free mammograms to underprivileged women nationwide—women for whom early detection would not otherwise be possible. Breast cancer is the leading cause of cancer deaths among women ages 40—55. Early detection is the key to survival, yet 13 million women in the U.S. over 40 have never had a mammogram.

With a simple, daily "click" at The Breast Cancer Site **(www. thebreastcancersite.com)**, you help provide mammograms to those in need. Mammography is the best-known method of early detection. And early detection is the key to a greater chance of survival and more treatment options.

The Rainforest Site **(www.therainforestsite.com)** was founded May 1, 2000 to help protect our environment. Visitors to The Rainforest Site save an area of rainforest with a simple click on the "Save Our Rainforests" button.

79.—THE TECH MUSEUM AWARDS—WWW.THETECH.ORG

When I first saw this organization and looked at their web site I saw that they were sponsoring the first ever award for using technology to transform the way we live.

Here is some information about the award to be announced in September.

From the web site:

The Tech Goes Global—50 Countries Represented

The Tech Museum of Innovation Awards program has attracted 380 nominations from 50 countries around the world. Since the public launch on March 8, 2001, The Tech, along with global outreach assistance from the United Nations Development Program, presenting sponsor Applied Materials, and other partners and sponsors have successfully spread the word about the new awards.

The Tech Museum Awards will honor individuals, companies, and organizations that are using technology to transform the way we live. In keeping with The Tech's mission, the awards will showcase the profound impact technological innovation can have when applied creatively to solve significant challenges in the areas of health, education, environment, economic development, and equality. Nominees are in the process of completing applications for the July 1st deadline.

The judging process will be conducted by the Center for Science, Technology, and Society at Santa Clara University. In September, up to five finalists in each category will be announced. All finalists will be honored at the November 1, 2001 Awards Gala, where one finalist in each category will receive a $50,000 cash prize.

Mission Statement

The Tech is an educational resource to engage people of all ages and backgrounds in exploring and experiencing technologies affecting their lives, and to inspire young people to become innovators in developing technologies of the future.

The Tech is a work in progress. Energy and enthusiasm that flows into The Tech from donors, members, and friends, continues to pour back out into our community. The Tech provides a bridge that links people with technology, acting as a catalyst to arouse and awaken the imaginations of visitors.

There is much to be accomplished and with your help we are steadily moving forward. We salute all our supporters for their commitment to education, to technology, to the future.

The Annual Fund

The Annual Fund for Education provides ongoing support to sustain the educational mission of The Tech Museum of Innovation. Individuals, Corporations, Foundations and Government agencies all work together to maintain The Tech as a national and international resource. Through exceptional education programs and hands-on learning, The Tech's main focus is on building science and technology literacy, and inspiring the young to become innovators and technology leaders of the future.

80.—Shape a Future That's Unknowable— www.uh.edu/engines

A fellow participant in the Landmark Education course, "Power and Contribution", sent email recommending a look at this site. If you are interested in how we shape a future that is completely unknowable a listen to the radio show and/or reading some of the referenced books could well be in your future?

From the web site:

Information about *The Engines of Our Ingenuity*

Written and hosted by John Lienhard and KUHF-FM, Houston, *The Engines of Our Ingenuity* tells the story of how our culture is formed by human creativity. The program uses the record of history to reveal the way art, technology, and ideas have shaped us. Episode topics range from cable cars to Civil War submarines, from the connection between Romantic poets and Victorian science to the invention of the bar code. The series is broadcast five days a week by over thirty National Public Radio affiliates nation-wide. It was first aired on NPR member station KUHF-FM Houston on Jan. 4, 1988. It was made available nationally, three months later. As of July 2, 2001, 1632 new episodes will have been aired. The producers of the show have been Don Ham during 1988, Ron Russak until Oct., 1994, Rick Nelson until the Fall of 1995, and Capella Tucker thereafter. *Engines* airs in Houston on KUHF-FM 88.7 at 7:35 AM and 3:55 PM, Monday through Friday. The theme music for the Radio series was created by Andrew Lienhard.

81.—PEERSPIRIT, INC.—WWW.PEERSPIRIT.COM

Carol Hidinger sent an email promoting this site. They have a newsletter, great wilderness adventure tours and they invite you to purchase books and to become part of their e-mail council and participate in their seminars, consulting, and adventures. So says Carol.

From the web site:

Greetings from PeerSpirit

PeerSpirit(TM), Inc. In Service to the Circle is a small educational company co-founded by Christina Baldwin and Ann Linnea, located in the state of Washington, USA.

The word "PeerSpirit" names the methodology developed by Baldwin in her book, **Calling the Circle, the First and Future Culture** (Bantam, 1998). Together, Baldwin and Linnea have created an accessible methodology that uses circle, or council, to foster clear communication and accountability in self-governing groups as diverse as family gatherings to corporate teams.
It is our firm belief that the ability to gather in face to face community-spirited groups is the skill most needed to respond creatively to the changes coming in the 21st Century.

It has taken us a long time to enter cyberspace with this philosophy. You who have found us here are invited to enter the circle of real time and space—to read Calling the Circle, to call circles into your own lives, to contact PeerSpirit, becoming part of our e-mail council and participating in our seminars, consulting, and adventures.

82.—AN HONEST ANSWER AND AN OPINION—*LISTEN* TO PEOPLE

When I started working on this book I sent an email to my address list soliciting ideas and comments.

Here is a response from Gerry, my stepdaughters' father.

I think it is self-explanatory and well thought out. There are opinions expressed and thinking people may have different opinions. Gerry has clearly put some thought into his opinions expressed here.

Thanks Gerry!

A professional reviewer responded to this item with the following:

"Why is one man's opinion—especially not the author's—injected in the middle of the book—particularly a man who says, "I am not a big fan of charities?" This seems to be a poor choice for trying to make the author's case of supporting charities."

Clearly I haven't made the point clearly that this book isn't about supporting charities. The point of the book is to take part in the solution. Supporting charities is one way to do that. It is not the only way, of course. Listening to others' viewpoints, acknowledging that their viewpoint is just as valid as yours, and continuing to work toward a world that works for everyone is another, perhaps even more effective, way to take part in the solution.

Thanks Reviewer!

From the email:

As you can see I am not one who responds immediately. I have thought about it and I will share my thoughts, but you may not want to use them.

I am not a big fan of charities. In many cases charities promise to provide life's needs but the dollars get lost in administrative salaries. That bothers me a bunch. Since I do not research the charities that do pass the bulk of the donations to the needy I classify them all into one category. Makes it easier that way.

However I do believe we all have a role to play in making this world a better place for everyone to live. It seems to me the best use of time and assets would be to help people help themselves. You know the thing about giving a man a fish and he eats for a day, but teach a man to fish and he eats forever.

The problem however, is that in today's society one can not provide for himself. The laws are too biased toward big business, the rich, and of course the powerful. The poor and lower middle class are stuck into what I call "social slavery". We have gone from a mostly farm economy, through the industrial revolution, and now the technological revolution. For people to survive in today's society, they must depend on a bigger entity, i.e. big business, big government, or whatever. When people rely on big business they are usually taken advantage of and forced to work for slave wages. Slave wages barely provide a family to survive so families encourage all members of the family to participate in the bread winning responsibility. Consequently, we have a huge problem with child labor throughout the third world countries.

The U.S. also plays a big role in this problem, because our big businesses would rather see big gains in the stock market than fulfilling on their responsibility in providing jobs for the American workers. Have you ever noticed how many clothes are made in the USA today? Most major clothing manufacturers today have their clothes made in the third world countries. In fact much of what we consume today comes from the third world countries where people are grossly underpaid, compared to American standards. This perpetuates the social slavery of the world. In the U.S.'s wisdom we even went so far as to pass an anti-labor law, NAFTA, to promote U.S. business in those countries.

Throughout the world, in my opinion, we have become less involved with people and survival, and more involved with profit. Unfortunately, I don't see an end to this in the near future. It seems to me the only cure for our dilemmas is a massive organizing effort to thwart the oppressive nature of the rich and powerful. We need to take a more active role in government, and indeed governments. Change our attitudes that big business is our friend. We need to help our neighbors, not just with money, but with time and caring. Anyway, I try to do this through empowering the poor.

I hope I made some sense!

83.—SWAMI BEYONDANANDA'S GUIDELINES FOR ENLIGHTENMENT—

If you are getting email you are probably, at least occasionally, getting one of those emails that people forward to a whole list from their email address book. One such email I got seemed worth adding to this book for a little humor—if you like this sort of thing.

From the email:

The Subject of the email—Wit and Wisdom
The content: SWAMI BEYONDANANDA'S GUIDELINES FOR ENLIGHTENMENT

"Drive your Karma; Curb your Dogma"

1. Be a fundamentalist—make sure the Fun always comes before the mental.

2. Realize that life is a situation comedy that will never be canceled. A laugh track has been provided.

3. Remember that each of us has been given a special gift, just for entering—so you are already a winner.

4. The most powerful tool on the planet is Tell-A-Vision. That is where I tell a vision to you and you tell a vision to me. That way, if we don't like the programming we're getting, we can simply change the channel.

5. Life is like photography. You use the negative to develop.

6. And, no matter what adversity you face, be reassured: Of course God loves you—she's just not ready to make a commitment.

7. It is true. As we go through life thinking heavy thoughts, thought particles tend to get caught between the ears, causing a condition called truth decay. So be sure to use mental floss twice a day.

8. And when you're tempted to practice tantrum yoga, remember what we teach in Swami's Absurdiveness Training class: "Don't get even, get odd."

9. If we want world peace, we must let go of our attachments and truly live like nomads. That's where I no mad at you, you no mad at me. That way, there'll surely be nomadness on the planet.

10. And peace begins with each of us. A little peace here, a little peace there, pretty soon all the peaces will fit together to make one big peace everywhere.

11. I know great earth changes have been predicted for the future, so if you're looking to avoid earthquakes, my advice is simple. When you find a fault, just don't dwell on it.

12. There's no need to change the world. All we have to do is toilet train the world, and we'll never have to change it again.

13. Everything I have told you is channeled. That way, if you don't like it it's not my fault.

14. And remember, enlightenment is not a bureaucracy. So, we don't have to go through channels.

15. Finally, if you are looking for the key to the universe, I have some bad news and some good news. The bad news is—there is no key to the universe. The good news is—it has been left unlocked.
    —Swami Beyondananda

84.—Woman With a New View of Culture—WWW.NYTIMES.COM (Wed., June 20, 2001—p.A8)

Thoraya Obaid, head of the United Nations Population Fund, is a Muslim woman from conservative Saudi Arabia. She seems to be an ideal person to lead the discussions by the General Assembly about AIDS. She is very much aware of the cultural differences and sensitivities that need to be included in the talks.
Good luck Ms. Obaid!

I looked at the nytimes.com web site, searched for "Thoraya Obaid" and, among several articles, this popped up:

From the web site:

FOREIGN DESK | June 20, 2001, Wednesday
Woman With a New View of Culture

By BARBARA CROSSETTE (NYT) 1138 words
Late Edition—Final, Section A, Page 8, Column 3

ABSTRACT—UN special session on fighting AIDS will highlight central role of Thoraya Obaid, Muslim woman from Saudi Arabia who heads UN Population Fund; agency that once dispensed family planning advice has become leading campaigner for safer sex; Obaid herself comes from one of conservative Arab countries that resist explicit wording on gay sex, women's rights and adolescent sexuality; she warns that conference participants must be sensitive to cultural differences; photo (M)

85.—POSITIVE FUTURES NETWORK—WWW.FUTURENET.ORG

Here is a web site, a non-profit organization, committed to a just, sustainable, and compassionate future.

From the web site:

About Positive Futures Network
The Positive Futures Network was founded in March 1996 based on the belief that humanity is in the midst of an historic transition. The industrial era, which brought tremendous increases in technical and scientific prowess, also brought a deepening social, economic, political and environmental crisis. Even as the crisis deepens, however, there is evidence that new understandings are emerging among millions of people regarding the need to affirm our relationship to the non-human world, to each other, and to the spiritual center of each individual. Yet people who have those understandings often complain of feeling isolated, overwhelmed, and unclear as to how to make a significant difference.

The Network's goal is to enhance the power of people working to create a more just, sustainable, and compassionate future by increasing their public visibility, their sense of interconnection, and their access to visions, tools, stories and techniques for change. To that end, the Network publishes YES! A Journal of Positive Futures, which combines analysis of key problems with news of actions people are taking in the United States and around the world to create a more positive future. Stories commonly report on similar actions in many places that reveal patterns that show the potential for significant social change.

This Web site augments the magazine's reach, providing additional information and links to relevant organizations. In addition, network staff and members of the board of directors and the editorial advisory team are frequent speakers at conferences and workshops related to systemic social change.

86—Ideals Work—www.idealswork.com

In my email one day I found a message about this web site and it was under construction. Since then the web site has blossomed. For those of us who espouse an ideal once in a while, maybe there is something going on here. Try it?

From the web site:

About IdealsWork

Ever wanted to change the world? Well, you're in the right place! IdealsWork was created by three friends who dreamed of making companies into better stewards of people, animals, and the planet.
IdealsWork makes it easy for you to find and support companies that share your values. We call it "flexing your ideals"—the powerful effect when each of us votes for a better world with every purchase we make.

Ever wonder...

about the social and environmental practices of the brands you buy—or whether there are other brands that treat the world better?

Now you can find out, instantly!

You can research a major purchase, like a car or a cd player, or more everyday items like soda or soap. Pretty much anything! What you get is a list of brands, sorted according to how they perform against your own unique standards. Think of IdealsWork as your own personal research service, available anytime.

It's free!

IdealsWork is completely, absolutely free. Plus, we will never, ever share any information you give us with anyone else. So put your ideals to work—and give IdealsWork a try!

87.—Social Entrepreneurship— www.Ashoka.org

Do you think of yourself as a social entrepreneur? You may just be one and you may qualify for support from this organization. I found an email one day (7/29/01) that pointed to this organization. Check it out!

Ashoka's Mission

Ashoka's mission is to develop the profession of **social entrepreneurship** around the world.

Ashoka invests in people. It is a global non-profit organization that searches the world for social entrepreneurs—extraordinary individuals with unprecedented ideas for change in their communities. Ashoka identifies and invests in these social entrepreneurs when no one else will. It does so through stipends and professional services that allow "Ashoka Fellows" to focus fulltime on their ideas for leading social change in education and youth development, health care, environment, human rights, access to technology and economic development. Ashoka has invested in more than 1,100 Ashoka Fellows in 41 countries. Those Fellows have transformed the lives of millions of people in thousands of communities worldwide.

Among the entrepreneurs Ashoka has backed is Rodrigo Baggio. With grant money from Ashoka, Rodrigo has trained almost 60,000 at-risk children with computer and Internet skills. His project, the Committee to Democratize Information Technology (CDI), created a network of more than 200 self-managed computer schools in the urban slums of 17 Brazilian states. Helping students who might otherwise have turned to drug trafficking or violence, Rodrigo is bridging the digital divide while providing important job opportunities to young Brazilians. His project is expanding exponentially as he opens schools in Japan,

Colombia, Mexico and Uruguay with partners like AOL, Microsoft, Starmedia and the InterAmerican Bank.

Origin of the Name

Who was Ashoka?
Ashoka was a 3rd Century B.C. Emperor of India who is remembered as one of the world's earliest and most impactful social innovators.

After uniting the Indian sub-continent (currently southeast Asia) by force, Ashoka was stricken with remorse and renounced violence.

Ashoka then dedicated the rest of his life to the peaceful promotion of social welfare, economic development, and tolerance for all religions. He instituted the region's first medical services, launched a vast well-digging program, and developed the first comprehensive infrastructure in southern Asia. Ashoka also planted thousands of shade trees along India's hot and dusty roads.

The organization Ashoka was founded in the spirit of Emperor Ashoka's extraordinary creativity, global-mindedness, and tolerance.

We elected our first Ashoka Fellows in India in 1982.

In Sanskrit, Ashoka means *"the active absence of sorrow"*.

What is a Social Entrepreneur?
Ashoka Fellows prove every day that the most powerful force for change in the world is a new idea in the hands of a leading social entrepreneur.

The job of a social entrepreneur is to recognize when a part of society is stuck and to provide new ways to get it unstuck. He or she finds what is not working and solves the problem by changing the system, spreading the solution and persuading entire societies to take new leaps. Social entrepreneurs are not content just to give a fish or teach how to fish. They will not rest until they have revolutionized the fishing industry.

Identifying and solving large-scale social problems requires a social entrepreneur because only the entrepreneur has the committed vision and inexhaustible determination to persist until they have transformed an entire system. The scholar comes to rest when he expresses an idea. The professional succeeds when she solves a client's problem. The manager calls it quits when he has enabled his organization to succeed. Social entrepreneurs go beyond the immediate problem to fundamentally change communities, societies, and the world.

Ashoka Fellow Veronica Khosa was frustrated with the system of health care in South Africa. A nurse by trade she saw sick people getting sicker, elderly people unable to get to a doctor and hospitals with empty beds that would not admit patients with HIV. So Veronica started Tateni Home Care Nursing Services and instituted the concept of "home care" in her country. Beginning with practically nothing, her team took to the streets providing care to people in a way they had never received it—in the comfort and security of their homes. Just years later, the government had adopted her plan and through the recognition of leading health organizations the idea is spreading beyond South Africa. Social entrepreneurs like Veronica redefine their field and go on to solve systemic social problems on a larger scale.

The past two decades have seen an extraordinary explosion of entrepreneurship and competition in the social sector. The social sector has discovered what the business sector learned from the railroad, the stock market and today's digital revolution: That nothing is as powerful as a big new idea—if it is in the hands of a first class entrepreneur.

In country after country the number of citizen organizations is up hundreds, often thousands-fold. Tiny Slovakia had a handful of such organizations in 1989 and now boasts more than 10,000. Of the approximately 2 million citizen sector organizations working in the United States, 70 percent of them were established in the last 30 years. Eastern Europe has seen more than 100,000 such organizations established in the seven years following the fall of the Berlin Wall.

The revolution—led by leaders like Veronica—is fundamentally changing the way society organizes itself and the way we approach social problems. These leaders are certainly doing more than giving a fish. They are teaching the world to swim.

Read more about social entrepreneurship

- *The Entrepreneur's Revolution and You*
  by William Drayton, President and Founder of Ashoka

- *The Meaning of "Social Entrepreneurship"*
  by J. Gregory Dees, Stanford University

Historical Examples of Leading Social Entrepreneurs

Susan B. Anthony (U.S.)—Fought for Women's Rights in the United States, including the right to control property and helped spearhead adoption of the 19th amendment.

David Brower (U.S.)—Environmentalist and conservationist, he served as the Sierra Club's first executive director and built it into a worldwide network for environmental issues. He also founded Friends of the Earth, the League of Conservation Voters and The Earth Island Institute.

Vinoba Bhave (India)—Founder and leader of the Land Gift Movement, he caused the redistribution of more than 7,000,000 acres of land to aid India's untouchables and landless. Mahatma Gandhi described him as his mentor

Frederick Law Olmstead (U.S.)—Creator of major urban parks, including Rock Creek Park in Washington DC and Central Park in NYC, he is generally considered to have developed the profession of landscape architecture in America

Mary Montessori (Italy)—Developed the Montessori approach to early childhood education

Some Present Day Social Entrepreneurs

Dr.Verghese Kurien (India)—Founder of the AMUL Dairy Project which has revolutionized the dairy industry through the production chain of milk, small producers, consumer products and health benefits

Bill Drayton (U.S)—Founded Ashoka, Youth Venture, and Get America Working!

Muhammad Yunus (Bangladesh)—Founder of microcredit and the Grameen Bank

Marian Wright Edelman (U.S.)—Founder and president of the Children's Defense Fund (CDF) and advocate for disadvantaged Americans and children

Ralph Nader (U.S.)—Fighting for consumer rights and working to increase citizen access to government

Michael Brown and Alan Khazie (U.S.)—Founders of City Year, a program to promote community service and civic participation among teenagers

88.—PROSPECTS FOR ECONOMIC GROWTH
WWW.WORLDBANK.ORG/PROSPECTS/

From the web site:

The World Bank's Development Prospects web site offers analysis and advice concerning the prospects for economic growth, world trade, financial flows, and primary commodities, the impact of global economic trends on the developing countries, and information about global and regional economic forecasts. The information is meant to help policymakers and their advisors anticipate and adapt to rapidly changing global economic trends.

Topics

Global Trends

Global Trends concerns the analysis and forecasting of developments in the international environment for developing countries, and for macroeconomic trends.

International Finance

Recent developments and prospects for capital flows to developing countries from private and official sources.

Global Commodities

Information, historical prices and price forecasts for major agricultural, energy and metals primary commodities.

For extensive information on our topics we developed a **targeted search**

89.—DEVELOPMENT AND THE ENVIRONMENT IN LATIN AMERICA
WWW.ECOAMERICAS.COM

From the web site:

EcoAméricas covers development and the environment in Latin America for an international audience of businesses, NGOs and public agencies.

It is published monthly by Fourth Street Press, an independent corporation in Santa Monica, California.

The goal of EcoAméricas is to provide continuing, clear-eyed coverage at a time when reporting on Latin American environmental issues has been piecemeal at best and too often biased by competing agendas.

Section VIII
Things to consider doing

90.—HOW ABOUT SOME INSIGHT? A STEP INTO THE FUTURE? WWW.HONDA2001.COM/MODELS/INSIGHT WWW.PRIUS.TOYOTA.COM

Some folks are interested is conserving the resources that are limited on this planet. Buckminster Fuller proposed use of renewable resources like solar power and wind power to make sure we never run out of the energy resources that we need to enjoy a relatively high quality of life. Petroleum resources may still be large but they are not renewable nor will they last forever.

One way to participate in the conservation of such resources is to use as little as possible. Our devotion to cars in the USA has become a way of life. The size of cars has grown recently as more and more of us drive vans or SUVs. We have an SUV that uses a gallon of regular gas to go 15 to 19 miles. We needed a second car to enjoy our American way of life so we went car shopping the other day. Diana has had her eye on the new VW Beetles for some time as they are an expression of "design" and she is in the beginning of a new career as an Interior Designer. We looked at the Beetles—lots of engineering details have been designed into that car. Oh yes, good gas mileage was one of our shopping criteria as we were getting more and more concerned about doing some part of the conservation of natural resources that seems needed. We were thinking at least 30 miles per gallon.

We looked at the small Toyotas, the Cabrio convertible, the Honda Civic (a great car), and the Honda Insight hybrid and the Toyota hybrid. The Toyota hybrid wouldn't be available for six months or it might be in our driveway. The bright red Insight was available to take home! It is rated at 60 to 70 miles per gallon—so far we are getting about 50mpg for the first 250 miles. It is a cute, modern looking car, I call it a "Step into the Future". The Insight now has well over 20,000 miles on it and has averaged over 50 mpg consistently. Now there is a hybrid Civic by Honda and many other makers are talking hybrids!

The December 2001 Reader's Digest (**www.rd.com**) includes an article titled "Lean, Green Driving Machine" on page 98. It is about the Insight and the Prius and what the auto companies are planning—like hybrid SUVs by 2003. Interesting! Hey, I filed our Insight with gas last night, reset one of the trip odometers which also tracks the mileage, and drove to Chicago (about 39 miles). When I got to the lot where I parked for the evening—I had averaged 72+miles per gallon (11/15/01).

91.—MAKE YOUR OPINION KNOWN—YOU CAN MAKE A DIFFERENCE

I just read this email and email exchange from my wife's cousin and his wife Mary. Steve and Mary have two sons who are dwarfed. One is their natural son, the other is adopted. Their family is a model family who take wonderful care of their children and do a great job of parenting. I am proud to be related to them.

I have edited the following email exchanges to give them a modicum of privacy.

Basically, if it's not obvious, the exchange came from a radio program (the "John Williams Show")—

Subj: **FW: advertising clip on John Williams show**
Date: 3/6/01 7:40:41 AM Central Standard Time
From:...(Stephen)
To:...multiple family members and (diana and lyle)
Just to let you know we're not powerless to create effective change in the world.

From: Mary...
Sent: Monday, March 05, 2001 10:09 PM
To: Manley, Todd
Cc: Rose, Mary June
Subject: Re: advertising clip on John Williams show
I'm very glad to hear you recognized that the promo was insensitive & pulled it. For that, I'll spare you the entire lecture I was mentally preparing & just give you the short version.
Please let Steve Cochran know that short statured people prefer the term 'dwarf' to 'midget'. I don't know why & I don't care why—but I think they are entitled to choose the politically correct term for themselves. If Steve ever chooses to discuss dwarfs on his show again, perhaps in a way that recognizes them as human, maybe he'll actually get

the terminology correct.

Thanks,

Mary

––––Original Message––––

From: Manley, Todd <TManley@tribune.com
<mailto:TManley@tribune.com>>

To: 'MGRZYWA

Cc: Rose, Mary June <MRose@tribune.com
<mailto:MRose@tribune.com>>

Date: Monday, March 05, 2001 12:52 PM

Subject: RE: advertising clip on John Williams show

Mary...that particular promo was prepared without much sensitiv-
ity, and I apologize for that. Please know that the clip has been
pulled from the air. Thank you for listening, and caring.

Todd Manley

Production Director/Asst. Program Director

WGN Radio

––––Original Message––––

From: Mary

Sent: Saturday, March 03, 2001 6:35 PM

To: MattBubala@wgnradio.com;
<mailto:MattBubala@wgnradio.com;>
AndyTarnoff@wgnradio.com;
<mailto:AndyTarnoff@wgnradio.com;>
SteveBuchman@wgnradio.com;
<mailto:SteveBuchman@wgnradio.com;>
DanFalato@wgnradio.com
<mailto:DanFalato@wgnradio.com>

Subject: advertising clip on John Williams show

Hi—

I recently heard a short clip on the John Williams show advertising one of the other shows—I think it was either Sports

Central or Steve Cochran. The clip in question was a discussion of a "midget" that was stalking Claudia Schiffer. Please let me know which show was promoting itself with this clip.
Thanks,
Mary

92.—IMPROVE YOUR FINANCIAL SITUATION—WWW.RICHDAD.COM

Recently a book was recommended to me. "Rich Dad, Poor Dad" written about a man who when a young lad of 9, began to be taught by his best friend's dad, the rich dad, and had those teachings to compare to what he was taught by his own father, poor dad. The book was very interesting to me. I think most of us would benefit from studying the book and our improved financial situations will help raise the economic level of the planet.

From the website:—this is a personal recommendation—not a commercial!

Robert Kiyosaki is the author of **Rich Dad, Poor Dad**. An international best seller; it explains what the rich teach their children about money, that the poor and middle class do not. *"The main reason people struggle financially is because they spent years in school but learned nothing about money. The result is, people learn to work for money…but never learn to have money work for them."* says Robert. Born and raised in Hawaii, Robert is fourth-generation Japanese American. He comes from a prominent family of educators. His father was the head of education for the State of Hawaii. After high school, Robert was educated in New York and upon graduation, he joined the U. S. Marine Corps and went to Vietnam as an officer and a helicopter gunship pilot.

Returning from the war, Robert's business career began. In 1977 he founded a company that brought to the market the first nylon and Velcro "surfer" wallets, which grew into a multi-million dollar world-wide product. He and his products were featured in ***Runner's World, Gentleman's Quarterly, Success Magazine, Newsweek***, and even ***Playboy***. Leaving the business world, he co-founded in 1985, an international education company that operated in seven countries, teaching business and investing to tens of thousands of graduates. His year-long television show was beamed across America on the Nostalgia Network, carrying his educational message. Retiring at age 47, Robert does what he loves best—investing. Concerned about the growing gap between the "haves" and "have nots", Robert created the game board CASHFLOW, which teaches the game of money, here before only known by the rich. Although Robert's business is real estate and developing small cap companies, his true love and passion is teaching. He has shared the speaking stage with such greats as **Og Mandino**, **Zig Ziglar**, and **Anthony Robbins**. Robert Kiyosaki's message is clear. "Take responsibility for your finances or take orders all your life. You're either a master of money or a slave to it." Robert holds classes that last from 1 hour to 3 days teaching people about the secrets of the rich. Although his subjects run from investing for high returns and low risk; to teaching your children to be rich; to starting companies and selling them; he has one solid earth shaking message. And that message is, **Awaken The Financial Genius** that lies within you. Your genius is waiting to come out. Most participants leave excited, some angry, but everyone is deeply moved. This is what world famous speaker and author **Anthony Robbins** says about Robert's work. "*Robert Kiyosaki's work in education is powerful, profound, and life changing. I salute his efforts and recommend him highly.*" During this time of great economic change, Robert's message is priceless.

CASHFLOW is a Registered Trademark of **Cashflow Technologies, Inc**. ©2000 1.800.308.3585 | phone info@richdad.com <mailto:info@richdad.com>| email

93.—A NEW TWIST ON
TITHING—WWW.NEWTITHING.ORG

Here's a guy who was in the "SPOTLIGHT" in the <u>Stanford</u> magazine, March/April 2001, p. 95. Claude Rosenberg, retired investment
strategist, launched a nonprofit service in 1998 called New Tithing
Group. the web site recommends ways to calculate how much to
donate and gives tips for maximizing tax savings from donations and
evaluating the efficiency of a given charitable organization. Rosenberg
practices what he preaches. Among other philanthropic activities, he
and his wife, Louise, founded the Center For Social Innovation at
Stanford's Graduate School of Business. "Philanthropy is not just giving—it's investing in the future of your family and your children", he
says.

Shouldn't we all, or at least those of us who can see it in our future,
generate the capability to found a foundation or two that will be
investments in our families' futures?
And if enough of us do so, don't you think we'll have a profound effect
on the future of the planet?

From the website:

<u>About NewTithing Group, Developer of *PrudentPal*</u>

<u>Background</u>
NewTithing Group is a non-profit organization founded by money
manager and philanthropist Claude Rosenberg to expand upon the
research of his 1994 book, Wealthy and Wise: How You and America
Can Get The Most Out of Your Giving" (Little, Brown).

<u>Mission</u>
NewTithing Group educates the public and their advisors to make
comfortably affordable charitable donations through sound budgeting.

Through its philanthropic research and planning tools, the Group strives to help individuals lead more meaningful lives with the knowledge that they are improving the public good at their own comfortable capacity: The Group believes that a comfortable donation makes a happier donor and a more effective charitable investor.

<u>Philosophy</u>
NewTithing Group's resources help people determine comfortably affordable donations based on factors such as: income, expenses (including debt), and investment assets (excluding personal homes and possessions). Yet determining how much to give to charity involves each donor's subjective comfort level. The Group thus assumes that the ancient custom of "tithing" still remains a constructive practice for people with income, yet little or no assets.

<u>Educational Resources</u>
The Group's educational resources include PrudentPal Charitable Giving Planner, an on-line budgeting tool; The New Guide to Comfortable Giving (a text-based complement to PrudentPal available at cost in hard copy format); and Proprietary IRS-Based Research on wealth and affordable donations, updated annually. The Group's resources are meant for donors, investors, financial/tax/philanthropic advisors, private foundations, corporate giving programs, and other interested entities.

which   can   be   found   here: **http://newtithing.org/frames/ f about01.html**, thank you.

94.—Go to Church!

Yesterday morning I attended Mass with my son in Park City, Utah. I was raised by Protestant missionaries as I may have mentioned previously. My participation in organized religious activities has been limited since my High School days and my current view is that I'll attend any service of any religion as long as they are open to visitors who are not committed to any single religion and someone invites me to participate.

My other son is married to a Jewish woman who has the family practicing many of the Jewish Traditions (he has now converted to Judaism himself). So my family includes, I think, a small example of the world's diverse religious practices.

As I listened to the priest's homily, and watched the practicing Catholics participate in the morning's service, I was also thinking about this book. My thoughts ranged over the basic principles that I see in the religions I have read about and watched to a limited extent. I'm certainly no expert, just a guy who wants us all to have economic freedom beyond the end of hunger! So, I think while the baptized Catholics are going up front to receive the Eucharist (is that the right word?), don't all the major religions really espouse the principles of treating each other as we would like to be treated, contribute to your fellow humans, and do others no harm? My friend, the executive director of the area Girls Scouts Council, says there are six core human values that all religions and ethical philosophies espouse:
1—Trustworthiness, 2—Respectfulness, 3—Responsibility, 4—Caring, 5—Citizenship, and 6—Fairness
If a person would get themselves in action around those six values from going to church wouldn't that be useful to participating in having the world work?

Some people might say, as I have, "but look at all the terrible things (wars etc.) people have done in the name of religion! Be that as it is, as

I look at what most religions (those I know a little about) teach, it is mostly basic human values. Some people, in my opinion, take some of their religion and carry it to unhealthy extremes, but that doesn't negate the value inherent in the system.

So, go to church! Look into what the church you attend teaches to find what God is telling you. Or, as some people do, create your own way of listening to God.

Recently I, and my beautiful wife, decided to start attending a church. Well, we may not go every week but we do want to attach ourselves to a spiritual community of some sort. As people who look at the many religions and churches that human-kind is currently engaged in or with and who see that most of them include much of the teachings and practices that seem to contribute to a world that works for everyone, we have chosen the Unitarian Universalist Church to attend and con-tribute to. It seems to be one that includes everyone and that inclusion is important to us as parents of a family that includes children of many faiths at this time.

95.—ORGANIZE AND/OR PARTICIPATE IN A CROP WALK—
WWW.CHURCHWORLDSERVICE.ORG

In 1976 I moved from Palo Alto California to DeKalb, Illinois. After moving with my two sons we stirred the community to start a youth soccer program. So I became the first regional commissioner for the DeKalb-Sycamore AYSO (American Youth Soccer Organization) program. Somehow, out of my involvement in the community that came from being the head of the soccer program, when the person who led the organizing of the annual CROP walks stepped down, I said I'd be the one to keep the walks going.

We changed the walk from a 10 mile walk to a 10K walk to attract more participants at one point I recall. However, the second year I was in charge and it was still a ten mile event, I was out for a run one morning and realized I could run ten miles. How would it be to run the CROP walk that year with a sign on my back that said "$100 per mile" and raise $1,000 as a contribution to what the CROP walks were all about (see below). I **did** run it that year. I **did** put that sign on my back. The following day the local paper had a picture of Lyle and Diana Smith (from behind) as they took off on a ten mile run for the CROP walk and Lyle had that sign on his back—"$100 per mile"!! A front page picture it was too!

From the web site:

CWS provides blankets and other tools of hope for their neighbors around the block—and around the world.
   Founded in 1946, Church World Service is the relief, development, and refugee assistance ministry of 36 Protestant, Orthodox, and Anglican denominations. Working in partnership with indigenous organizations in more than 80 countries, CWS supports sustainable self-help development, meets emergency needs, aids refugees, and helps address

the root causes of poverty and powerlessness. ***Within the United States***, Church World Service assists communities in responding to disasters, resettles refugees, promotes <u>fair national and international policies</u>, provides <u>educational resources</u>, and offers opportunities to join a people-to-people network of local and global caring through participation in **CROP WALKS,** the <u>TOOLS OF HOPE & BLANKET Program</u>, and the <u>"Gift of the Heart" Kit Program</u>. ...*let us love, not in word or speech, but in truth and action.*—I John 3:18

96.—LOVE YOUR FAMILY! INCLUDING THOSE YOU DON'T KNOW ABOUT?

I went to the Post Office the other day and by the fullness of the parking lot I knew I'd be in for a wait. Usually I have a book to read in the car with me but that day nothing. So, I said to myself, I'll write something. Maybe I'll think of something for the book?
As I walked toward the lobby for waiting in line for service, I scanned the contents of wastebaskets for something to write on. I saw a nice big envelop with plenty of white space—there is a use for junk mail!

Here is what I wrote about "Love Your Family."

Here's something that doesn't happen every day. Or, even to very many of us ever! When I was a young man (maybe not yet a *man*) I lived with a couple that my parents had asked to be sort of "house parents" while they went back to Africa (Congo) again. They were missionaries in the Congo and had been going back and forth for nearly 30 years. I was in college at the time, living at home, about 19 or 20 years old. I got to know this couple pretty well, the wife better than the husband, as you'll soon see.
Some four years later I was between girlfriends and the wife and I somehow had some time together that was pretty intimate. We both knew we shouldn't be that intimate and at the same time we liked each other a lot and did what we did.

Time went by, I got married, we moved to California, we had two sons, and life went on. There was a period in Switzerland, Colorado, and then back to California. Eighteen years later, as I was just about to move to Illinois with the two sons, leaving my alcoholic (by then) wife behind, I had occasion to spend a couple hours with my good friend from years back. I had heard that her husband had been killed in a farm accident several years earlier and that she had remarried. I thought we could meet and tie a ribbon around our relationship, to say the "farewell" that I felt had been left off years before, and to wish each other a nice life. I flew to LA for the day and we met for a couple hours. Just before I left that encounter to move on, she showed me a photo of a son—she said he was mine! There were no requests, it was a secret from others, and she just wanted me to know. Given the secret, it didn't seem to me to that I should do anything about the son I didn't know I had. So I did nothing.

Well, Time went on, a son asked genetic questions about brown eyes from blue eyed parents and eventually he was told the truth. I, in the meantime, was unaware until I got an email from one of my alma maters asking if it would be OK to give my email address to a woman who's now deceased mother was a friend of mine back in the late 1950s. I did not recognize the woman's name, first or last. I wondered who it could be and I said sure, give her my email. I was flattered that someone from my past had remembered me enough to want to be in touch through a daughter. Some chapters of my life seem so far away and long ago compared to my current life. I left for a week in Montana (see # 3).

After a week in Montana, following 1025 bicycle riders who were raising money for AIDS Vaccine research, I came home to email from my son's sister! She and his wife had traced me through a web site that has my photo, and biography and were asking if I would be open to contact. The son, at this point did not know that they had found me but was at least interested in his/my medical history. Fair enough!

I replied, sure, let's talk. And, the emails started flying back and forth over the thousand plus miles between us.

I wondered if he, his wife, his five children, and his sisters would even like me. I hoped they would.

I wondered if they would resent me in any way. I hoped not. He said the past is the past. An enlightened attitude!

So what was there to do? I saw that what there was to do was love my family. Now that it had expanded there was more family to love.

Any expectations? No, it's best to leave these (new) relationships open to whatever we make of them.

Love life!

Love your family!!

PS A visit to Austin, TX has since had us meet each other and spend a couple days getting to know each other. As it turns out, we like each other a lot, the son has a great family with five home-schooled children ages 6 through 20. We will stay related!

97.—Teen Connect—
WWW.TEENCONNECTINC.COM

So, there I was sitting on the throne reading the *Reader's Digest* and an article about "Teen Heroes" jumped out at me. Alfred used to have phone conversations with his grandmother, even after Alzheimer's took her away bit by bit. She died when he was 13. A year after his grandmother died, Alfred, knowing that different generations gained much by being in touch, founded **Teen Connect**, a program linking teenagers and seniors by telephone. Alfred is now connected with Selma Kahan who is 79. Over 200 other teenagers are connected with seniors such as Lindsey Kurland, 17 and Max Silverstein, 100 on April 2001. To start a **Teen Connect** chapter, visit the web site.

From the web site:

Teen Connect
"Students in Service to Seniors"

Introduction

Teen Connect, an approved community service project and proposed school club at Pine Crest School, is an intergenerational project that matches high school students to older isolated elderly in our community. The idea was proposed by the project coordinator and founder of the proposed club, Alfred Ciffo III, a student at Pine Crest School. The project is a win-win opportunity for both the high school student volunteers and the seniors they serve. Teen Connect volunteer members contact homebound, isolated older people by phone, which reduces their loneliness; and, student volunteers learn about issues of aging, civic responsibility, and the importance of caring for all people regardless of age or disability. The members of the advisory council propose to create a Teen Connect club.

Purpose

The purpose of Teen Connect is to help reduce the negative consequences of aging for isolated Seniors by providing telephone contact with interested high school student volunteers. The project provides an avenue for students to help solve community service problems through volunteerism. This can be an independent study project and class administered by faculty advisors and others.

National Need

For example, in our locale approximately one third of residents in Broward County are over 65 years of age. In Broward County, according to the Department of Elder Affairs, approximately 97,000 people over the age of 65 live alone. In 1998, it was estimated that 42,000 of these people have difficulty performing basic activities of daily livid, and are isolated from social interaction. In 1999, the State of Florida Department of Elder Affairs Strategic Plan for 1999-2004 has set goals that include: (1)Helping elders age in place (in their own residences). (2)Helping elders maintain their ability to function properly. And (3)Helping elders reduce isolation.

If you see a similar need in your community consider starting a chapter.

Starting a Chapter

There has been considerable interest in Teen Connect over the past several months. A number of schools have started organizing chapters. They are: Coral Springs High SchoolOrganizer: **Lindsey Kurland**, and David Posnack Hebrew Day SchoolOrganizer. Eli Damatov

By starting a Teen Connect chapter, could you think of a more wonderful way to have interschool communication while doing good in your community? We think not! If you are interested in more information please contact:

Alfred F. Ciffo III or **Anthony Belotto** Email: **teenconnct@aol.com**

Activities

Student volunteers are solicited to make weekly phone calls to older individuals. The students receive an orientation which includes but is not limited to: issues of aging, confidentiality; roles and responsibilities; emergency issues, communication styles; inappropriate conversations, and project evaluation. The students meet on a regular basis and have the opportunity to hear community speakers and discuss issues regarding their telephone contacts. Emergency telephone contacts for adult advisors are provided to every student.

Advisory Council

The project encompasses a Service-Learning model. The Advisory Council consists of a teacher advisor, a community based volunteer organization representative, and parents. The advisory group serves to approve Teen Connect guidelines, support student activities, provide development information; and intervene in any inappropriate subject matter, or difficult situations.

Community Service Hours

Student volunteers document volunteer hours on a log, which is maintained, for future reference. As the project develops, volunteer names will be considered for various recognition's both local and nationwide.

Teacher Advisor

A faculty advisor is necessary to supervise and administer class meetings. The class will meet approximately two times a month. Students will learn how to converse with elders as well as gain insight into their lives. Students learn about issues and consequences of aging while expanding their knowledge of social concerns. The instruction will facilitate conversation between the youth and the elderly. In that way, older individuals gain a friendly contact that helps reduce isolation and its consequences; and stimulates cognitive thinking.

Working Together

Teen Connect has developed a relationship with a social service organization, Broward Grandparents, and its executive director Ruth Marx. By working with your school, social service organizations, and teen members, success is inevitable in making a difference in our communities by helping seniors.

98.—Try the Landmark Forum— www.landmarkeducation.com

Landmark Education provides what they call non-linear educational opportunities. I have been partaking of their offerings since Landmark was formed in 1991 and recommend that anyone interested in creating their own future—take a look!

From the web site:

A fundamental principle of Landmark Education's work is that people—and the communities, organizations, and institutions with which they are engaged—have the possibility not only of success, but also of fulfillment and greatness. The ideas, insights, and distinctions on which Landmark's programs are based make Landmark a leader and innovator in the field of training and development.

In **independent research**, graduates of Landmark's programs report major positive results in the following areas:

- The quality of their relationships.

- The confidence with which they conduct their lives.

- The level of their personal productivity.

- The experience of the difference they make.

- The degree to which they enjoy their lives.

Quick Fact

Top100expo.com ranks The Landmark Forum second only to space travel on its Top100 Adventures list, calling it an **extraordinary and unprecedented adventure**.

99.—EARTH CHARTER—
WWW.EARTHCHARTER.ORG

Someone pointed me to this web site and it turns out to be quite interesting. Take a look! I have copied quite a bit from the web site for you. As I look at this I see it really is about **having the world work for everyone!**

From the web site:

The Earth Charter is an authoritative synthesis of values, principles, and aspirations that are widely shared by growing numbers of men and women in all regions of the world. The principles of the Earth Charter reflect extensive international consultations conducted over a period of many years. These principles are also based upon contemporary science, international law, and the insights of philosophy and religion. Successive drafts of the Earth Charter were circulated around the world for comment and debate by nongovernmental organizations, community groups, professional societies, and international experts in many fields.

Origin and history of the Earth Charter

In 1987 the United Nations World Commission on Environment and Development issued a call for creation of a new charter that would set forth fundamental principles for sustainable development. The drafting of an Earth Charter was part of the unfinished business of the 1992 Rio Earth Summit. In 1994 Maurice Strong, the Secretary General of the Earth Summit and Chairman of the Earth Council, and Mikhail Gorbachev, President of Green Cross International, launched a new Earth Charter initiative with support from the Dutch government. An Earth Charter Commission was formed in 1997 to oversee the project and an Earth Charter Secretariat was established at the Earth Council in Costa Rica.

Mission of the Earth Charter Initiative

A new phase in the Initiative began with the official launching of the Earth Charter at the Peace Palace in The Hague on June 29, 2000. The mission of the Initiative going forward is to establish a sound ethical foundation for the emerging global society and to help build a sustainable world based on respect for nature, universal human rights, economic justice, and a culture of peace.

Objectives of the International Earth Charter Initiative are:

- To disseminate the Earth Charter to individuals and organizations in all sectors of society throughout the world.

- To promote the educational use of the Earth Charter in schools, universities, faith communities, and a variety of other settings, and to develop and distribute the necessary supporting materials.

- To encourage and support the use, implementation, and endorsement of the Earth Charter by civil society, business, and government at all levels.

- To seek endorsement of the Earth Charter by the United Nations in 2002, the tenth anniversary of the Rio Earth Summit.

(I thought I'd copy a portion of the Charter itself to give you the flavor—decided to copy in the whole thing. It is available in 26 different lauguages! From Arabic to Thai!)

The Earth Charter Document

PREAMBLE

We stand at a critical moment in Earth's history, a time when humanity must choose its future. As the world becomes increasingly interdependent and fragile, the future at once holds great peril and great promise. To move forward we must recognize that in the midst of a magnificent diversity of cultures and life forms we are one human family and one Earth community with a common destiny. We must join together to bring forth a sustainable global society founded on respect for nature, universal human rights, economic justice, and a culture of peace. Towards this end, it is imperative that we, the peoples of Earth, declare our responsibility to one another, to the greater community of life, and to future generations.

Earth, Our Home
Humanity is part of a vast evolving universe. Earth, our home, is alive with a unique community of life. The forces of nature make existence a demanding and uncertain adventure, but Earth has provided the conditions essential to life's evolution. The resilience of the community of life and the well-being of humanity depend upon preserving a healthy biosphere with all its ecological systems, a rich variety of plants and animals, fertile soils, pure waters, and clean air. The global environment with its finite resources is a common concern of all peoples. The protection of Earth's vitality, diversity, and beauty is a sacred trust.

The Global Situation
The dominant patterns of production and consumption are causing environmental devastation, the depletion of resources, and a massive extinction of species. Communities are being undermined. The benefits of development are not shared equitably and the gap between rich and poor is widening. Injustice, poverty, ignorance, and violent conflict are widespread and the cause of great suffering. An unprecedented rise in human population has overburdened ecological and social systems. The foundations of global security are threatened. These trends are perilous—but not inevitable.

The Challenges Ahead
The choice is ours: form a global partnership to care for Earth and one another or risk the destruction of ourselves and the diversity of life. Fundamental changes are needed in our values, institutions, and ways

of living. We must realize that when basic needs have been met, human development is primarily about being more, not having more. We have the knowledge and technology to provide for all and to reduce our impacts on the environment. The emergence of a global civil society is creating new opportunities to build a democratic and humane world. Our environmental, economic, political, social, and spiritual challenges are interconnected, and together we can forge inclusive solutions.

Universal Responsibility

To realize these aspirations, we must decide to live with a sense of universal responsibility, identifying ourselves with the whole Earth community as well as our local communities. We are at once citizens of different nations and of one world in which the local and global are linked. Everyone shares responsibility for the present and future well-being of the human family and the larger living world. The spirit of human solidarity and kinship with all life is strengthened when we live with reverence for the mystery of being, gratitude for the gift of life, and humility regarding the human place in nature.

We urgently need a shared vision of basic values to provide an ethical foundation for the emerging world community. Therefore, together in hope we affirm the following interdependent principles for a sustainable way of life as a common standard by which the conduct of all individuals, organizations, businesses, governments, and transnational institutions is to be guided and assessed.

PRINCIPLES

I. RESPECT AND CARE FOR THE COMMUNITY OF LIFE

1. Respect Earth and life in all its diversity.

a. *Recognize that all beings are interdependent and every form of life has value regardless of its worth to human beings.*

b. *Affirm faith in the inherent dignity of all human beings and in the intellectual, artistic, ethical, and spiritual potential of humanity.*

2. Care for the community of life with understanding, compassion, and love.

a. *Accept that with the right to own, manage, and use natural resources comes the duty to prevent environmental harm and to protect the rights of people.*

b. *Affirm that with increased freedom, knowledge, and power comes increased responsibility to promote the common good.*

3. Build democratic societies that are just, participatory, sustainable, and peaceful.

a. *Ensure that communities at all levels guarantee human rights and fundamental freedoms and provide everyone an opportunity to realize his or her full potential.*

b. *Promote social and economic justice, enabling all to achieve a secure and meaningful livelihood that is ecologically responsible.*

4. Secure Earth's bounty and beauty for present and future generations.

a. *Recognize that the freedom of action of each generation is qualified by the needs of future generations.*

b. *Transmit to future generations values, traditions, and institutions that support the long-term flourishing of Earth's human and ecological communities.*

In order to fulfill these four broad commitments, it is necessary to:

II. ECOLOGICAL INTEGRITY

5. Protect and restore the integrity of Earth's ecological systems, with special concern for biological diversity and the natural processes that sustain life.

a.   *Adopt at all levels sustainable development plans and regulations that make environmental conservation and rehabilitation integral to all development initiatives.*

b.   *Establish and safeguard viable nature and biosphere reserves, including wild lands and marine areas, to protect Earth's life support systems, maintain biodiversity, and preserve our natural heritage.*

c.   *Promote the recovery of endangered species and ecosystems.*

d.   *Control and eradicate non-native or genetically modified organisms harmful to native species and the environment, and prevent introduction of such harmful organisms.*

e.   *Manage the use of renewable resources such as water, soil, forest products, and marine life in ways that do not exceed rates of regeneration and that protect the health of ecosystems.*

f.   *Manage the extraction and use of non-renewable resources such as minerals and fossil fuels in ways that minimize depletion and cause no serious environmental damage.*

6. Prevent harm as the best method of environmental protection and, when knowledge is limited, apply a precautionary approach.

a.   *Take action to avoid the possibility of serious or irreversible environmental harm even when scientific knowledge is incomplete or inconclusive.*

b. *Place the burden of proof on those who argue that a proposed activity will not cause significant harm, and make the responsible parties liable for environmental harm.*

c. *Ensure that decision making addresses the cumulative, long-term, indirect, long distance, and global consequences of human activities.*

d. *Prevent pollution of any part of the environment and allow no build-up of radioactive, toxic, or other hazardous substances.*

e. *Avoid military activities damaging to the environment.*

7. Adopt patterns of production, consumption, and reproduction that safeguard Earth's regenerative capacities, human rights, and community well-being.

a. *Reduce, reuse, and recycle the materials used in production and consumption systems, and ensure that residual waste can be assimilated by ecological systems.*

b. *Act with restraint and efficiency when using energy, and rely increasingly on renewable energy sources such as solar and wind.*

c. *Promote the development, adoption, and equitable transfer of environmentally sound technologies.*

d. *Internalize the full environmental and social costs of goods and services in the selling price, and enable consumers to identify products that meet the highest social and environmental standards.*

e. *Ensure universal access to health care that fosters reproductive health and responsible reproduction.*

f. *Adopt lifestyles that emphasize the quality of life and material sufficiency in a finite world.*

8. *Advance the study of ecological sustainability and promote the open exchange and wide application of the knowledge acquired.*

a.   *Support international scientific and technical cooperation on sustainability, with special attention to the needs of developing nations.*

b.   *Recognize and preserve the traditional knowledge and spiritual wisdom in all cultures that contribute to environmental protection and human well-being.*

c.   *Ensure that information of vital importance to human health and environmental protection, including genetic information, remains available in the public domain.*

III. SOCIAL AND ECONOMIC JUSTICE

9. *Eradicate poverty as an ethical, social, and environmental imperative.*

a.   *Guarantee the right to potable water, clean air, food security, uncontaminated soil, shelter, and safe sanitation, allocating the national and international resources required.*

b.   *Empower every human being with the education and resources to secure a sustainable livelihood, and provide social security and safety nets for those who are unable to support themselves.*

c.   *Recognize the ignored, protect the vulnerable, serve those who suffer, and enable them to develop their capacities and to pursue their aspirations.*

10. *Ensure that economic activities and institutions at all levels promote human development in an equitable and sustainable manner.*

a.   *Promote the equitable distribution of wealth within nations and among nations.*

b. *Enhance the intellectual, financial, technical, and social resources of developing nations, and relieve them of onerous international debt.*

c. *Ensure that all trade supports sustainable resource use, environmental protection, and progressive labor standards.*

d. *Require multinational corporations and international financial organizations to act transparently in the public good, and hold them accountable for the consequences of their activities.*

11. Affirm gender equality and equity as prerequisites to sustainable development and ensure universal access to education, health care, and economic opportunity.

a. *Secure the human rights of women and girls and end all violence against them.*

b. *Promote the active participation of women in all aspects of economic, political, civil, social, and cultural life as full and equal partners, decision makers, leaders, and beneficiaries.*

c. *Strengthen families and ensure the safety and loving nurture of all family members.*

12. Uphold the right of all, without discrimination, to a natural and social environment supportive of human dignity, bodily health, and spiritual well-being, with special attention to the rights of indigenous peoples and minorities.

a. *Eliminate discrimination in all its forms, such as that based on race, color, sex, sexual orientation, religion, language, and national, ethnic or social origin.*

b. *Affirm the right of indigenous peoples to their spirituality, knowledge, lands and resources and to their related practice of sustainable livelihoods.*

c. *Honor and support the young people of our communities, enabling them to fulfill their essential role in creating sustainable societies.*

d. *Protect and restore outstanding places of cultural and spiritual significance.*

IV. DEMOCRACY, NONVIOLENCE, AND PEACE

13. Strengthen democratic institutions at all levels, and provide transparency and accountability in governance, inclusive participation in decision making, and access to justice.

a. *Uphold the right of everyone to receive clear and timely information on environmental matters and all development plans and activities which are likely to affect them or in which they have an interest.*

b. *Support local, regional and global civil society, and promote the meaningful participation of all interested individuals and organizations in decision making.*

c. *Protect the rights to freedom of opinion, expression, peaceful assembly, association, and dissent.*

d. *Institute effective and efficient access to administrative and independent judicial procedures, including remedies and redress for environmental harm and the threat of such harm.*

e. *Eliminate corruption in all public and private institutions.*

f. *Strengthen local communities, enabling them to care for their environments, and assign environmental responsibilities to the levels of government where they can be carried out most effectively.*

14. Integrate into formal education and life-long learning the knowledge, values, and skills needed for a sustainable way of life.

a.   *Provide all, especially children and youth, with educational opportunities that empower them to contribute actively to sustainable development.*

b.   *Promote the contribution of the arts and humanities as well as the sciences in sustainability education.*

c.   *Enhance the role of the mass media in raising awareness of ecological and social challenges.*

d.   *Recognize the importance of moral and spiritual education for sustainable living.*

15. Treat all living beings with respect and consideration.

a.   *Prevent cruelty to animals kept in human societies and protect them from suffering.*

b.   *Protect wild animals from methods of hunting, trapping, and fishing that cause extreme, prolonged, or avoidable suffering.*

c.   *Avoid or eliminate to the full extent possible the taking or destruction of non-targeted species.*

16. Promote a culture of tolerance, nonviolence, and peace.

a.   *Encourage and support mutual understanding, solidarity, and cooperation among all peoples and within and among nations.*

b.   *Implement comprehensive strategies to prevent violent conflict and use collaborative problem solving to manage and resolve environmental conflicts and other disputes.*

c. *Demilitarize national security systems to the level of a non-provocative defense posture, and convert military resources to peaceful purposes, including ecological restoration.*

d. *Eliminate nuclear, biological, and toxic weapons and other weapons of mass destruction.*

e. *Ensure that the use of orbital and outer space supports environmental protection and peace.*

f. *Recognize that peace is the wholeness created by right relationships with oneself, other persons, other cultures, other life, Earth, and the larger whole of which all are a part.*

THE WAY FORWARD

As never before in history, common destiny beckons us to seek a new beginning. Such renewal is the promise of these Earth Charter principles. To fulfill this promise, we must commit ourselves to adopt and promote the values and objectives of the Charter.

This requires a change of mind and heart. It requires a new sense of global interdependence and universal responsibility. We must imaginatively develop and apply the vision of a sustainable way of life locally, nationally, regionally, and globally. Our cultural diversity is a precious heritage and different cultures will find their own distinctive ways to realize the vision. We must deepen and expand the global dialogue that generated the Earth Charter, for we have much to learn from the ongoing collaborative search for truth and wisdom.

Life often involves tensions between important values. This can mean difficult choices. However, we must find ways to harmonize diversity with unity, the exercise of freedom with the common good, short-term objectives with long-term goals. Every individual, family, organization, and community has a vital role to play. The arts, sciences, religions, educational institutions, media, businesses, nongovernmental organizations, and governments are all called to offer creative leadership. The partnership of government, civil society, and business is essential for effective governance.

In order to build a sustainable global community, the nations of the world must renew their commitment to the United Nations, fulfill their obligations under existing international agreements, and support the implementation of Earth Charter principles with an international legally binding instrument on environment and development.

Let ours be a time remembered for the awakening of a new reverence for life, the firm resolve to achieve sustainability, the quickening of the struggle for justice and peace, and the joyful celebration of life.

100.—A PUBLISHING WEB SITE FOR ANYONE TO SELF-PUBLISH FOR THE WORLD WWW.INDYMEDIA.ORG

As you can see from the material copied from the web site, this is a place to publish articles that don't appear in the "main stream" media.

From the web site:

ABOUT INDYMEDIA

about indy | **imc allies** | **contact us** | **what's new?** | **stories about imc**

The Independent Media Center is a network of collectively run media outlets for the creation of radical, accurate, and passionate tellings of the truth. We work out of a love and inspiration for people who continue to work for a better world, despite corporate media's distortions and unwillingness to cover the efforts to free humanity.

History

The **Independent Media Center (www.indymedia.org)**, was established by **various independent and alternative media organizations and activists** in 1999 for the purpose of providing grassroots coverage of the **World Trade Organization (WTO)** protests in Seattle. The center acted as a clearinghouse of information for journalists, and **provided up-to-the-minute reports**, **photos**, **audio** and **video** footage through its website. Using the collected footage, the **Seattle Independent Media Center (seattle.indymedia.org)** produced a series of **five documentaries**, uplinked every day to **satellite** and distributed throughout the United States to public access stations.

The center also produced its own newspaper, distributed throughout Seattle and to other cities via the internet, as well as hundreds of audio segments, transmitted through the web and Studio X, a 24-hour micro and internet radio station based in Seattle. The site, which uses a democratic open-publishing system, logged more than 2 million hits, and was featured on America Online, Yahoo, CNN, BBC Online, and numerous other sites. Through a decentralized and autonomous network, hundreds of media activists setup independent media centers in London, Canada, Mexico City, Prague, Belgium, France, and Italy over the next year. IMCs have since been established on every continent, with more to come.

For more information, see the IMC **Frequently Asked Questions**

101.—IMPROVE A NEIGHBORHOOD (SEE TIME MAGAZINE ARTICLES 10/16/00 AND 7/16/01)
WWW.TIME.COM

In TIME magazine (10/16/00) I found a brief article by Carole Buia, titled "Here Comes the Neighborhood". This presents a different slant on the timeworn phrase—"here goes the neighborhood" does it not?

Richmond McCoy had developed the largest real estate management firm controlled by an African American but that was not enough for this man. He began helping churches develop property in poor neighborhoods. This led to UrbanAmerica, the first real estate Investment Company to focus on distressed urban areas, a market sinfully ignored by most money men.

And another article by Carole
From the www.time.com web site:

"July 16, 2001
A prodigal son returns home to find profit in preserving his country's precious resources
BY CAROLE BUIA
His workday sometimes finds John Forgach draped in mosquito netting, paddling the backwaters of the Amazon in a dugout canoe. He's on the hunt—for a new investment. Forgach, 52, spent decades making money the old-fashioned way, as an investment banker in places like Geneva and New York City. Now he is back in his native Brazil to show that preserving the environment and indigenous cultures can be profitable. As CEO of a Sao Paulo-based private company called A2R Environmental Funds, Forgach raises money from institutions like the Swiss government and the World Bank Group and invests mainly in sustainable agriculture and food processing in Latin America, includ-

ing the Amazon. If you've bought organic raspberries under General Mills' Cascadian Farm label or ordered hearts of palm in a European restaurant during the past year, you've probably done business with A2R.

..."

102.—HOST SOMEONE FROM ANOTHER COUNTRY— WWW.HEARTLANDINTERNATIONAL.ORG

In October 2000, we hosted two women from Russia. Since then we have also hosted two women from Tanzania. We are still in contact with one of the Tanzanian women on a regular basis.

Heartland International is a non-profit organization in Chicago dedicated to sharing information and training with non-profit organizations in other countries. They work in particular with the Ukraine, Russia and Belarus. The funding is provided through grants and fundraising. The participants are invited to Chicago for three weeks at Heartland's expense to study and learn different methods to manage and make successful their non-profit organizations in their home countries.

From the web site:

Heartland International is non-profit organization based in Chicago, Illinois. Established in 1989, the organization designs, implements, and manages political, economic and social development projects, as well as international education exchange programs.

Through its programs, Heartland International seeks to:

- bring to bear the traditionally underutilized resources of the Midwestern United States on international programs;

- act as a catalyst in strengthening emerging democratic institutions;

- provide training and technical assistance to encourage microenterprise development;

- support the role of women in economic, political and social affairs in emerging democracies;

- provide a forum for the exchange of ideas between the U.S. and foreign policymakers;

- promote mutual understanding between various segments of U.S. society and their international counterparts.

103.—HAVE A PARTY! (FUNDRAISING EVENTS)

I just received an email from the ski club where I used to work. One of the members is a member of an organization, the "Bolingbrook Business and Professional Women's Organization", which is putting on a fund-raising event "with a Delicious Buffet Dinner and a Cash Bar". Tickets are $25 per person and the proceeds go for battered women, for shelters, for scholarships for women, and for the DuPage County Junior Miss program. The shelters are in surrounding communities. Local businesses have also donated items that will be auctioned off at the event.

Lyle's Myles and Diana's Smyles is another example of a party that is a fund-raiser for a cause. On November 12th in Naperville, IL several dozen people will be walking or running or riding 6.6 kilometers (or a portion thereof) to raise money for World Runners who are assisting east African communities better themselves. After the 6.6 K is over they will be partying and eating to celebrate! PS—in 2000 the event raised over $2,000.

And now it's 2001 and the next Lyle's Myles is almost upon us. This year it is on Sunday November 11th.

From the Runner's World web site:

Details about: Lyle's Myles & Diana's Smyles

Date:	Sunday, November 11, 2001
Name:	Lyle's Myles & Diana's Smyles
City, State:	Naperville,IL

Events

Distance 1:	6.7K Run	**Start Time 1:**	2:30 PM
Distance 2:	6.7K Walk	**Start Time 2:**	2:30 PM

Other Information

Event Attributes:	Multi-sport Charity Benefit RW-Sponsored
Estimated Event Size:	100
Highlights:	The 6.7 Kilometer event (run/walk/watch)is followed by a social eating birthday celebration

Contact Information

Contact:	Lyle smith
	1918 Springside Circle
	Naperville,IL 60565
	Phone: (630)-416-8520
	Email <u>dsslbs@aol.com</u>

And see number 105 also.

PS The 2001 event is now complete—we raised over $2,300 and had a blast!
And, the fastest male runner (unfortunately he was disqualified by the rules—he crossed before Lyle), came from Alabama. He is in the service, stationed in Alabama, and just happened to be visiting in the Illinois area for the weekend and wanted to race!

104.—WHOLE FAMILY CAN MAKE A DIFFERENCE
WWW.MAKEADIFFERENCEDAY.COM

"The family that volunteers together stays together." This line comes from an article in the Naperville *Daily Herald* on October 3, 2000. The article is pointing out that October 28, 2000 is the 10th annual "Make a Difference Day". Some of the suggested activities: collect food for the needy, clean up the yard of a senior, reading to the blind, or do some other good deeds.

The fourth Saturday in October each year is the annual makeadifferenceday.

From the web site (10/16/01):

First Lady urges action
In a Public Service Announcement now appearing on TV, First Lady Laura Bush says, "To the hundreds of thousands of Americans who have volunteered in recent weeks, thank you. To the thousands more who still want to know what they can do, October 27 is Make A Difference Day. Take a minute, an hour, or the entire day, and mentor a child, work a food bank, or simply offer a word of kindness. You'll find you can make all the difference in the world."

105.—RUN A RACE!
WWW.WORLDRUNNERS.ORG
AND WWW.RUNNERSWORLD.COM

For example, on October 29, 2000 the Sycamore Pumpkin Festival "Pumpkin Race" started at 9:35 am. This race is sponsored annually by the Greater Sycamore Chamber of Commerce. See www.sycamorechamber.com

Other races are held for fund raising to support a myriad of causes. Lyle's Myles and Diana's Smyles was run on November 12, 2000 and again on November 11, 2001 for the eighth time. The ninth running is November 10th, 2002. This event supports "World Runners"; an organization committed to the advancement of health, prosperity, and peace in the communities of the world.

From the web site: www.worldrunners.org

Welcome to World Runners
World Runners is an organization of runners committed to the advancement of health, prosperity, and peace in the communities of the world. We raise funds by running for pledges. The focus in the year 2001 is on health and education of children.

Santa Rosa, California, August 17, 1999
Global Partners for Development, an international non-profit organization founded in 1978, today announced the reinstatement of World Runners for the purpose of expanding it's mission to broaden participation and bring about the end of hunger worldwide. The World Runners charter embraces the mission of Global Partners for Development and provides opportunity for people to participate in making a difference in the advancement of health, prosperity and peace worldwide through running, walking and related events.

Over its 20 year history, World Runners has become known for its numerous worldwide events resulting in these memorable milestones:

December 31, 1999—January 1, 2000 Millennium Runs—As a first expression of World Runners new existence, 12 millennium runs were produced in 5 countries.

Moscow Peace Marathons—in the middle to late '80s—1000 runners raising $2,000,000 in support of organizations ending world hunger

Save the Children Relays—25,000 participants raising funds for the immunization of 100,000 children against fatal childhood diseases

Transcontinental relay—runners carried a Save the Children message throughout the U.S., and ten other nations, gaining support from national, state and local governments

Other major fundraising campaigns including the New York and Boston Marathons, and other major marathons and smaller events that produced over $4 million for community projects and enrolled 13,000 members in 50 countries

About Global Partners for Development

Founded in 1978, Global Partners for Development is an international non-profit organization committed to the end of hunger throughout the world. It promotes that human life is sacred, that all people have the right to have their basic needs met, and that in a world with sufficient resources, hunger anywhere is unacceptable. Global Partners works in partnership with local community organizations in East Africa to address the underlying causes of chronic persistent hunger. The organization works to empower and bring forth worldwide recognition of the equality of women, provide resources and skills for basic survival, promote self sufficiency and education, foster committed action and personal involvement. The organization is based in Santa Rosa, California. For more information, please call (707) 579-5009 or visit http://www.gpfd.org.

From the web site: www.runnersworld.com

Race Calendars
Here's where you can find marathon calendars and a searchable database of all the races in our system. Special note to race directors: This is also the place to enter your race (for free) into our race calendar, and to sign up for our free Runner's World race sponsorship program.

106.—MAKE DEBORAH'S WISH COME TRUE—INSTEAD OF SPENDING ENERGY ON OUR DIFFERENCES SPEND IT ON SOMETHING PRODUCTIVE. WWW.GAYRIGHTS.ORG

Dateline—Naperville, IL—10-10-2000
(***Daily Herald,*** **Section 3, page 1)**

This morning when I picked up the paper a headline caught my eye. "GAY: Why didn't I have 'normal' feelings like my friends?" This article, written by a ***Daily Herald*** reporter, Deborah Kadin, actually addressed two issues. As a Jew, Deborah experienced the discrimination that most Jews are subjected to even today. Secondly, she finally "came out" both to herself and to others about being gay when she was 51 years old! Fifty-one years old!! She raises the issue at the end of her article that occurred to me as I read through the story of her life. Here is her final paragraph:

"But just as straight people don't have to declare their sexual orientation to the world, it's my wish that gays would not have to do so either. I would hope that someday all people could actually believe that we are all the same and yet we're all unique. Wouldn't it be nice if we could all just be!"

Deborah, I heartily agree with you! Furthermore, wouldn't it be nice if we all transferred the energy we spend on our differences to resolving issues such as making sure we are all fed, all clothed and all housed adequately? Wouldn't it be nice if the time and energy we waste on those differences was used to create an economically supportive world-wide culture in which we can all experience economic freedom above and beyond the end of hunger!

So, this opportunity is for each of us to make Deborah's wish come true. Transfer any tendency we have to spend time and energy on differences that do not matter or that should be honored and celebrated, to activities that support the economic freedom of all of us.

From the web site: www.gayrights.org

Human Rights Record of the World
Imagine living in a nation that upholds your human rights, and the human rights of all people. Imagine being governed by layers of government that secure and defend your human rights. For hundreds of millions of human beings, this kind of nation remains only a distant dream, the shadow of a shadow.

Many countries are vehemently hostile, coldly silent, or inactively supportive, toward implementing human rights protection. Some nations endlessly spout notions of equality, freedom and justice, yet the connection between rhetoric and reality is dangerously thin, as millions of their own people experience the unfulfillment and violation of human rights every second of every day.

The peaceful patience of the gay-allied community in the face of such human rights violations remains absolutely god-like. In a world that too frequently resorts to brutality to solve violations, this commitment to civility is undervalued and often misinterpreted as a weakness. Yet, even our patience has its limits. The Rule of Law is important only when laws do not violate human rights. Here you will find an easy to read-and-compare worldwide human rights chart to see who is fulfilling their obligations.

Human rights defenders in **organizations** around the globe are working tirelessly to make civilization a better place for all.

Gay people are 3-10% of Earth's population, meaning the human family contains 185.5 million—618.4 million gay men, women, and children. If gay individuals united to create a country, it would be the 5th to 3rd largest nation on Earth (note: current studies so far indicate 6-

8%, meaning 371 million—494.7 million human beings, or the 3rd largest nation on Earth).

107.—ASSIST A FOOD BANK E.G.
WWW.CHICAGOSFOODBANK.ORG

Recently we received in the mail another solicitation for money. This one was from the Greater Chicago Food Depository that helps hungry people get the nutritious food they need. This organization is involved in distributing more than 60,000 meals every day to over 585 soup kitchens, shelters and pantries. In 1999 more than 32 million pounds of food were provided! 35% of those hungry people served by this program are children.

Contributions are tax-deductible.

From the web site:

The Food Depository is…
a not-for-profit food distribution center working to feed hungry people in Cook County. The Depository is committed to efficiently distributing donated and purchased food through qualified agencies such as soup kitchens, shelters and pantries. Since its start in 1979, the Depository has remained steadfast to this mission.

The Food Depository is…
one of the largest food banks in the country, distributing nutritious food to more than 309,000 <u>different</u> adults and children in Cook County annually. Last year the Food Depository distributed 36.1 million pounds of food, valued at more than $54 million—that's the equivalent of 74,400 meals a day, 365 days a year.

The Food Depository is…
a source of healthy food for 600 member agencies, including soup kitchens, shelters, senior centers and food pantries.

The Food Depository is…
121,000 square feet of warehouse space where food is inspected and sorted before distribution. To see firsthand how it all works, call for a

tour at (773) 247-3663.
Greater Chicago Food Depository
4501 South Tripp Avenue
Chicago, Illinois 60632
Tel: 773/247-FOOD(3663)
Fax: 773/247-4232
Email: fooddepository@gcfd.org

108.—Pray for Peace
WWW.WORLDPUJA.ORG

Perhaps this spiritual; approach is one that you are interested in participating with. Take a look at the web site and see for your self if it looks like something for you to take action toward.

On November 12th, 2000, people were invited to join in on **www.worldpuja.org** for a live worldwide vigil to focus on lasting peace in the Middle East. At **http://emisaryoflight.com/om_prayers.htm** there is a description of the effort to give one million prayers for peace for the Middle East.

On Friday November 16th, 2001 there was a live global webcast at the beginning of Ramadan.

From the web site:

Our Purpose and Mission
WorldPuja was established in 1998 with the intent to use the power and global reach of the Internet for the expressed purpose of planetary healing. We offer free global webcasts where people from around the world gather to pray for world peace. These global meditations are broadcast live and are freely accessed in virtually all parts of the world. Combining the ancient power of prayer with the speed and global reach of the Internet allows us to link humanity in a unique and profound way. We have had people in 83 countries, on all 6 continents gather together online in prayer. Transcending religious and cultural differences, coming together in common intent and purpose, one global family.

A Response to the Need of our Time

Why WorldPuja?

A Time of Awakening—Mother Earth is waking up in a profound way. 1998 and beyond will present quantum levels of new awakening calling forth new levels of responsiveness and opportunity for our awakening OneHumanSpirit brothers and sisters everywhere. Dissemination of strategic spiritual information that reinforces daily life is key to the success of our planet and the people on it.

Using the Powerful Inner Technologies Together:
The power of praying and meditating together, of focusing attention with intention in-groups has been well documented. It is time to provide the opportunity for people throughout the world to come together, to harness the power of the inner technology of meditation and prayer. To do so has profound implications to the very direction that our future will take.

Profound Teachers, Knowledge, and Experience are Available Now—Brilliant, visionary thinkers-teachers-mentors representing many disciplines and cultures have delved deep into their individual areas of expertise, deep into their own inner experience and guidance and have collated profound knowledge and consciousness-shifting practices to be shared. These teachers and the body of expertise they represent can have a profound influence in facilitating personal growth and awakening-consciousness-shifting on our planet. Localized events and seminars reaching tens or hundreds of people in one area are fast becoming inadequate and inefficient. It is time to expand the communications paradigm to reach thousands of people simultaneously, worldwide.

We have created WorldPuja in response to the current need of our times. Imagine being connected around the planet in a WorldPuja Earth Pulse, using the power of inner AND outer technology to make a difference in the world. Imagine getting online and attending a Global Interactive Forum, hearing the latest information from key spiritual teachers and millennium thinkers. Long distance and just-in-time learning may be the only way we can stay updated in our vast and changing world consciousness.

We have created the basic infrastructure. Now it is up to you, our many brothers and sisters around the planet. Let us come together in this great experiment. Let us love and support each other as we traverse these amazing times. We invite you to visit often. Come to pray, to be in community, to contribute and make miracles happen.

109.—A CHARITABLE GIVING POOL
PHILANTHROPY.COMWWW.COF.ORG

No, it's not a swimming pool, it's a pool of charitable funds designed in a way that allows us to take the deduction now and make the gift later. An article in the November 2000 issue of "Bloomberg Personal Finance" on page 45 describes this method of charitable giving. There are over 500 community foundations nationwide. A couple pointers to information are: Chronicle of Philanthropy **philanthropy.com** Council on Foundations **www.cof.org** And, for example, Fidelity's Charitable Gift Fund **www100.charitablegift.org**

From the Council On Foundations web site:

Vision Statement

In an environment of unprecedented change and potential, the Council on Foundations in the twenty-first century supports philanthropy worldwide by serving as

A trusted *leader*

Promoting the highest values, principles and practices to ensure accountability and effectiveness in philanthropy.

An effective *advocate*

Communicating and promoting the interests, value and contributions of philanthropy.

A valued *resource*

Supporting learning, open dialogue and information exchange about and for philanthropy.

A respectful *partner*

Collaborating within a network of philanthropic and other organizations working to promote responsible and effective philanthropy.

From the philanthropy.com web site:

The Chronicle of Philanthropy is the newspaper of the nonprofit world. It is the No. 1 news source, in print and online, for charity leaders, fund raisers, grant makers, and other people involved in the philanthropic enterprise.

In print, *The Chronicle* is published biweekly except the last two weeks in June and the last two weeks in December (a total of 24 issues a year). A subscription includes full access to this Web site and news updates by e-mail—all at no extra charge. An online-only subscription is also available.

The Web site offers the complete contents of **the new issue,** an archive of **articles from the past two years,** and more than four years' worth of **grant listings**—all fully searchable.

Much of this material is available only to *Chronicle* subscribers. See the information below to find out how you can subscribe or, if you are already a subscriber, how you can register to use this valuable service.

For information on which portions of the site are free and which are restricted you our subscribers, please see our **site map.** Stories from the new issue are posted every other week, at 9 a.m. U.S. Eastern time, on the Monday preceding *The Chronicle's* issue date. The job announcements are updated on the Monday following the issue date.

110.—BE A CITIZEN OF THE WORLD AND WEAR THE T-SHIRT JUDYBLAKE@MSM.COM AND, WWW.WORLDCITIZEN.ORG

Declare yourself to be a citizen of the world. Since I was born to missionary parents who traveled back and forth across the Atlantic every four years or so and took their children along for the ride, and since I later lived in Switzerland for two years and three months and visited much of Europe while there, and then took a two month trip to return to the USA the long way around the planet, I have been fortunate to see a lot of the planet's countries and peoples and do see myself as a citizen of the world. To declare that in a way now popular in the US, I have ordered my T-shirt that says "I am a citizen of the World". Judy Blake can supply you with such a T-shirt also. Send her email at **judyblake@msm.com** and she will send you the address to which to send your $20 for a T-shirt of your very own! I'm sure she will share with you what happens to the portion of the $20 that isn't the cost of the shirt.

Just to see what would be there I just typed in **www.worldcitizen.org** and found the following. Here too is an opportunity to make a difference.

From the web site: www.worldcitizen.org

World Citizen Foundation

The World Citizen Foundation is a nonpartisan nonprofit organization dedicated to the proposition that all levels of political authority derive their legitimacy only from the fundamental sovereignty of the people.

This is widely accepted at local and national levels but not internationally or globally. This dichotomy is the ultimate source of the corruption of democracy at local and national levels, as the non-democratic paradigm which rules in international relations corrodes the paradigm of individual rights and freedom which is used domestically.

We believe that democracy is a human invention and a political "technology" which historically is still very young and whose potential has not been fully realized. As a human invention, it is imperfect and will always be but it is also perfectible. It is our duty to try to constantly improve democracy, and to see how it can be used to solve global problems.

We believe that global constitutional democracy and the concept of a world constitutional republic are options which ought to be explored to solve international and global issues.

Global trends in all walks of life show that public trust and accountability to public opinion is the most powerful weapon in the world today. Unfortunately, this accountability still does not exist in the maybe the most important arena of all: international politics.
An obsolete international system based on diplomacy and the idiosyncrasies of personal likes and dislikes of leaders determine war and peace and prevent the resolution of problems affecting billions.

The fact that global problems cannot be solved within a system of national states is one reason why Right and Left are locked in sterile and ultimately counter-productive debates.

The idea that all human beings have natural and inalienable rights that ought to be constitutionally protected should appeal to most if not all people. Logic dictates that if we accept that, then such constitutional protection ought to exist for all people, hence the need for a global constitution specifying fundamental rights and responsibilities.

The challenge is to determine in as intellectually rigorous a manner how this is possible, how to involve the people, how to build accountability in the system rather than an optional extra.

To explore these issues and promote the concepts of world democracy and world citizenship are the goals of the World Citizen Foundation.

Please join us in implementing these goals.

And...

Speech by Troy Davis, President, World Citizen Foundation

Stockholm speech
Democracy Forum 2000

Democracy and Poverty: a Missing Link?
Organized by International IDEA, the World Bank and the UN Development Programme
Stockholm, 8-9 June 2000

Is global democracy the missing link to solve global poverty?

Speech by Troy Davis, President, World Citizen Foundation Secretary of the Global Coalition World Democracy 2010 Lunch speaker, Friday 9 June 2000

This is an interesting speech, I think. Check it out.
http://www.worldcitizen.org/resources/speech.html

111.—SUPPORT THE AMERICAN FRIENDS SERVICE COMMITTEE WWW.AFSC.ORG

A while ago I sent out one of our periodic emails/letters asking friends and relatives for their money for one of our causes. My cousin Lauretta wrote back to say that she has chosen the AFSC as her target for donations. It deserves mention for sure and perhaps you might think it belongs in Section III? Well, here it is:

From the web site:

(The peace quote is changed weekly.)
It isn't enough to talk about peace; one must believe in it. And it isn't enough to believe in it; one must work at it.
—Eleanor Roosevelt (1951)
from **The Little Book of Peace**

About AFSC

The American Friends Service Committee (AFSC) is a Quaker organization that includes people of various faiths who are committed to social justice, peace, and humanitarian service. Its work is based on the Religious Society of Friends (Quaker) belief in the worth of every person, and faith in the power of love to overcome violence and injustice.

Founded in 1917 to provide conscientious objectors with an opportunity to aid civilian victims during World War I, today the AFSC has programs that focus on issues related to economic justice, peace-building and demilitarization, social justice, and youth, in the United States, and in Africa, Asia, Europe, Latin America, the Middle East, and at the United Nations (Geneva and New York).

Mission Statement

The American Friends Service Committee is a practical expression of the faith of the Religious Society of Friends (Quakers). Committed to the principles of nonviolence and justice, it seeks in its work and witness to draw on the transforming power of love, human and divine.

We recognize that the leadings of the Spirit and the principles of truth found through Friends' experience and practice are not the exclusive possession of any group. Thus, the AFSC draws into its work people of many faiths and backgrounds who share the values that animate its life and who bring to it a rich variety of experiences and spiritual insights.

This AFSC community works to transform conditions and relationships both in the world and in ourselves which threaten to overwhelm what is precious in human beings. We nurture the faith that conflicts can be resolved nonviolently, that enmity can be transformed into friendship, strife into cooperation, poverty into well-being, and injustice into dignity and participation. We believe that ultimately goodness can prevail over evil and oppression in all its many forms can give way.

Section IX
Things to join

112.—JOIN THE JAYCEES!
WWW.USJAYCEES.ORG

The Jaycees are the Junior Chamber of Commerce organizations. I recently received in my mail a flyer from the Illinois Jaycees requesting a donation. I sent them a check. Their flyer says: WE BELIEVE: "…That Earth's greatest treasure lies in human personality; and that service to humanity is the best work of life." You can call the Illinois Jaycees at (800) 472-4880.

Try the web site **www.usjaycees.org** from there you can find more information:

From the web site:

ABOUT THE JAYCEES
The United States Junior Chamber (Jaycees) gives young people between the ages of 21 and 39 the tools they need to build the bridges of success for themselves in the areas of business development, management skills, individual training, community service, and international connections.

Established in 1920 to provide opportunities for young men to develop personal and leadership skills through service to others, the Jaycees later expanded to include women, reflecting the growing influence and leadership of women in America.

For the past 81 years, Jaycees have been a force for good in America and around the world.

FOR MORE INFORMATION
To learn more about getting involved with this unique organization, visit the website at: **www.usjcees.org** or contact the national service center at: 1-800-**JAYCEES**

113.—JOIN A ROTARY CLUB
WWW.ROTARY.ORG

The international Rotary is large and widespread. Rotarians do amazing things through their local clubs. We know many people who participate in the local Rotary and have attended meetings occasionally as guests.

From the web site:

East Timor is 164th Rotary Country

About Rotary

Rotary is an organization of business and professional leaders united worldwide who provide humanitarian service, encourage high ethical standards in all vocations, and help build goodwill and peace in the world. In more than 160 countries worldwide, approximately 1.2 million Rotarians belong to more than 30,000 Rotary clubs.

Rotary club **membership** represents a cross-section of the community's business and professional men and women. The world's Rotary clubs meet weekly and are nonpolitical, nonreligious, and open to all cultures, races, and creeds.

The main objective of Rotary is service—in the community, in the workplace, and throughout the world. Rotarians develop community service projects that address many of today's most critical issues, such as children at risk, poverty and hunger, the environment, illiteracy, and violence. They also support programs for youth, educational opportunities and international exchanges for students, teachers, and other professionals, and vocational and career development. The Rotary motto is *Service Above Self.*

Although Rotary clubs develop autonomous service programs, all Rotarians worldwide are united in a campaign for the global eradication of polio. In the 1980s, Rotarians raised US$240 million to immunize the children of the world; by 2005, Rotary's centenary year and the target date for the certification of a polio-free world, the **PolioPlus** program will have contributed US$500 million to this cause. In addition, Rotary has provided an army of volunteers to promote and assist at national immunization days in polio-endemic countries around the world.

The Rotary Foundation of Rotary International is a not-for-profit corporation that promotes world understanding through international humanitarian service programs and educational and cultural exchanges. It is supported solely by voluntary contributions from Rotarians and others who share its vision of a better world. Since 1947, the Foundation has awarded more than US$1.1 billion in humanitarian and educational grants, which are initiated and administered by local Rotary clubs and districts.

114.—THE LIONS CLUBS
WWW.LIONSCLUBS.ORG

Since 1917, Lions have served the world's population through hard work and commitment to make a difference in the lives of people everywhere. With 1.4 million members serving in more than 44,600 clubs in 189 countries and geographical areas, Lions Clubs International is the world's largest service club organization. Lions are recognized worldwide for their service to the blind and visually impaired.

More From the web site:

Lions International Objects

- **To Create** and foster a spirit of understanding among the peoples of the world.

- **To Promote** the principle of good government and good citizenship.

- **To Take** an active interest in the civic, cultural, social and moral welfare of the community.

- **To Unite** the clubs in the bonds of friendship, good fellowship and mutual understanding.

- **To Provide** a forum for the open discussion of all matters of public interest; provided, however, that partisan politics and sectarian religion shall not be debated by club members.

- **To Encourage** service-minded people to serve their community without personal financial reward, and to encourage efficiency and promote high ethical standards in commerce, industry, professions, public works and private endeavors.

Lions Code of Ethics

- **To Show** my faith in the worthiness of my vocation by industrious application to the end that I may merit a reputation for quality of service.

- **To Seek** success and to demand all fair remuneration or profit as my just due, but to accept no profit or success at the price of my own self-respect lost because of unfair advantage taken or because of questionable acts on my part.

- **To Remember** that in building up my business it is not necessary to tear down another's; to be loyal to my clients or customers and true to myself.

- **Whenever** a doubt arises as to the right or ethics of my position or action towards others, to resolve such doubts against myself.

- **To Hold** friendship as an end and not a means. To hold that true friendship exists not on account of the service performed by one another, but that true friendship demands nothing but accepts service in the spirit in which it is given.

- **Always** to bear in mind my obligations as a citizen to my nation, my state, and my community, as to give them my unswerving loyalty in word, act, and deed. To give them freely of my time, labor and means.

- **To Aid** others by giving my sympathy to those in distress, my aid to the weak, and my substance to the needy.

- **To Be Careful** with my criticism and liberal with my praise; to build up and not destroy.

Section X
Things to click on

115.—CLICK ON
WWW.THEHUNGERSITE.COM
DAILY AND DONATE FREE FOOD

This can become a habit that provides a cup of food for someone each day. The site includes information about how many of us have clicked and how much food that has generated. Thehungersite.com sponsors pay for the food. The site puts out an on-line newsletter periodically too. On Oct. 11, 2000 the newsletter included this report from Uganda:

"HOW YOUR CLICKS HELP HOMELESS CHILDREN IN UGANDA
An estimated 1.3 million Ugandan children have been orphaned as a
Result of poverty, conflict or AIDS. Many of these children end up
Living on the streets without access to adequate food. Hunger,
Combined with a lack of education prevents them from attending school
Or finding decent jobs and they are forced to resort to begging,
theft or prostitution to survive.

Your clicks on The Hunger Site are helping The World Food Pro-gramme
(WFP) to distribute the proper food and nutrition to some of these
Children so that they can attend school or skills training, and
Ultimately, break the vicious cycle of poverty. To date, your support
Has already helped provide $200,000 of nutritious meals to orphan-ages
And training centers in Uganda. Thank you for making a difference!"

On the web site you'll see where you can click on "Spread the Word". If you click there you'll see this:

From the web site:

Tell 10 Friends Today!

24,000 people will die from hunger today. That's why it's so important to click daily and tell others about The Hunger Site.

Tell 10 friends about this fast, free way to fight world hunger, and you'll increase the number of lives we can touch. The Hunger Site has helped people in most desperate need; earthquake victims in El Salvador, those left adrift in war-torn Eritrea, families on the brink of starvation in drought-stricken North Korea, and many more. Your support enables The Hunger Site to continue its role as a powerful force in the fight against hunger. We greatly appreciate your efforts to spread the word.

Send an email today!

Simply fill in the email addresses of the people you'd like to tell (separated by commas), give us your email address, and hit "send." We'll take it from there! We respect the privacy of the information you give us and will not use this process to store any email addresses.

To continue helping The Hunger Site with every email you send, feel free to add our URL (**http://www.thehungersite.com**) to the signature block of your outgoing messages.

On the site you can find the giving history from all the clicks we do. In 1999. 2000 and 2001 the results are below.

Year	Clicks	Cups of Food	Kilograms	Metric Tons	Pounds
2001	43,728,058	44,147,417	2,503,397	2,503	5,518,566
2000	95,604,534	167,564,354	9,501,806	9,502	20,945,544
1999	25,994,473	52,983,557	3,004,480	3,004	6,662,947

The site also keeps track of your individual giving history. Ours, as of today 9-26-02:

Your giving history:

1 this week; 2 in the last 7 days
13 this month; 17 in the last 30 days
128 this year; 159 since June 15th, 2001.

116.—Donate free Mammograms by clicking on WWW.THEBREASTCANCERSITE.COM

The Hunger Site, the Breast Cancer Site, and The Rain Forest Site are all linked together. You can go to any of the three and you will have direct click access to the other two. And a fourth site the Animal Rescue site is there too! My wife says the mammogram procedure must have been invented by a man as it is quite uncomfortable to say the least. I read that a female comedian said the procedure sounds like putting something in a flat envelop and mailing it somewhere—that hurts! Nonetheless, the procedure is supposed to be very effective and worth doing even though there have been controversial reports in the news this year (2002). So, join me in daily clicking on…
www.thebreastcancersite.com

From the web site:

Tell 10 Friends Today!
43,000 women will die from breast cancer this year. That's why it's so important to click daily and tell others about The Breast Cancer Site.
By telling 10 friends about this fast, free way to fund mammograms for underprivileged women, you increase the number of women who will receive the gift of early detection. We've generated funds to provide hundreds of women with mammograms. With your help, we can have an even bigger impact in 2001.

Send an email today!
Simply fill in the email addresses of the people you'd like to tell (separated by commas), give us your email address, and hit "send." We'll take it from there! We respect the privacy of the information you give us and will not use this process to store any email addresses.

To continue helping The Breast Cancer Site with every email you send, feel free to add our URL (**http://www.thebreastcancersite.com**) to the signature block of your outgoing messages.

DAILY RESULTS

Breast cancer is the leading cause of cancer deaths among U.S. women ages 40-55, and is second only to lung cancer in the number of resulting cancer deaths. During the year 2001, 182,000 women will be diagnosed and 43,300 women will die of breast cancer. Early detection is the key to survival.

Your click on the "Fund Free Mammograms" button helps fund mammography screenings for underprivileged women who otherwise wouldn't receive the gift of early breast cancer detection. Mammograms are provided by the **National Breast Cancer Foundation**, who puts special emphasis on reaching low-income, minority, and working-poor women whose awareness of breast cancer and opportunity for help is often limited.

At The Breast Cancer Site, every day is a new opportunity to make a difference in the fight to prevent breast cancer deaths. The number of women helped depends on the number of visitors to The Breast Cancer Site. Please remember to click every day, and spread the word to family and friends.

117.—Favorite Bookmarks of some Stanford People e.g. www.google.com

As an alumnus of Stanford University I get the Stanford Magazine each month (I think I'm paying for it). In one issue I found an article listing the favorite bookmarks of some of the professors. Google, which I'd heard about but not used consistently, is now one of my frequently used sites.

From an article in the Stanford Magazine:
http://www.stanfordalumni.org/news/magazine/home.html

(I just used **www.google.com** to locate the Stanford Magazine however I could not retrieve the particular article that I had previously seen about these web sites.)

Terry Winograd, professor of computer science **www.google.com**

Our Mission Google's mission is to organize the world's information, making it universally accessible and useful.

Company Profile Google focuses exclusively on delivering the best search experience on the World Wide Web. Through innovative advances in search technology, Google helps users find the information they're looking for quickly and effectively. The company delivers services through its own web site at **www.google.com**, and by licensing its search technology to commercial sites.

And **www.cpsr.org CPSR's mission** CPSR is a public-interest alliance of computer scientists and others concerned about the impact of computer technology on society. We work to influence decisions regarding the development and use of computers because those decisions have far-reaching consequences and reflect our basic values and priorities. As technical experts, CPSR members provide the public and policymakers with realistic assessments of the power, promise, and limitations of computer technology. As concerned citizens, we direct public attention to critical choices concerning the applications of computing and how those choices affect society. Every project we undertake is based on five principles:

- We foster and support public discussion of, and public responsibility for decisions involving the use of computers in systems critical to society.

- We work to dispel popular myths about the infallibility of technological systems.

- We challenge the assumption that technology alone can solve political and social problems.

- We critically examine social and technical issues within the computer profession, both nationally and internationally.

- We encourage the use of information technology to improve the quality of life. CPSR is a democratically organized membership organization. Our accomplishments result from the active involvement of our members, supported by the CPSR staff and computer professionals across the country.

Andrea Lunsford, professor of English has these favorite web sites: History of Rhetoric **http://humanities.byu.edu/rhetoric/silva.htm** It may be a while before this science (mostly) major gets into this one.

Digital Future Coalition **www.dfc.org** The Digital Future Coalition (DFC) is committed to striking an appropriate balance in law and public policy between protecting intellectual property and affording public access to it.

James Montoya, vice provost for student affairs has as one of his favorite web sites, **www.political.adcritic.com** He says this is a must site for political enthusiasts.

118.—LINKS TO CHARITIES AT WWW.RD.COM

I was reading through the Reader's Digest one day and found an article that referenced the web site and all the links that could be found there. So here they are:

From the web site:

<u>**Only In America**</u>

You've read about the creative ways organizations are trying to raise money through sponsorships in the November 2001 issue of *Reader's Digest*. Now check out these links to find out how to contribute to the charities mentioned in "Just Don't Call Me Mommy."

Sponsor a covered bridge in New Hampshire:
http://www.tmclark.com/Bridges/bridges.html

Adopt an Egyptian animal mummy:
http://www.animalmummies.com

Contribute to clearing of minefields:
http://www.adoptaminefield.com

Adopt a bison: http://nature.org/adoptabison/help/index.html

Adopt a whale: http://www.whalecenter.org

Adopt a turkey: http://www.farmsanctuary.org

Adopt a wolf: http://www.defenders.org

Adopt a bat: http://www.batcon.org

Adopt hissing cockroaches: http://www.fonz.org/getinv/adopt.htm

Section XI
How will we know how we are doing? Is the condition of planet Earth and its inhabitants improving?

119.—RESULTS <u>WWW.RESULTSUSA.ORG</u>

This web site represents a non-profit, grassroots citizen's lobby that identifies sustainable solutions to the problems of hunger and poverty, in our world and in the U.S., and works to generate the resources necessary to make those solutions succeed. Actually this web site is more about how to get results than reporting on results.

From the web site:

RESULTS Successes in 2001

International Issues
Foreign Aid Dollars to Fight Tuberculosis

We were successful in getting more resources for international tuberculosis control. Deliberating the 2002 foreign aid funding bill, the House passed the Brown-Wilson-Morella-Andrews-Green amendment, which transferred an additional $20 million to international TB programs from agencies of the World Bank and the Asian Development Bank. This brought TB funding in the House bill up to $90 million bilaterally, plus $20 million within the new Global Fund to Fight AIDS, TB and malaria, for a total of $110 million. The Senate then passed an amendment, sponsored by Sens. Hutchison (R-TX) and Inouye (D-HI), to increase U.S. bilateral aid for TB from $70 million to $80 million.
The final 2002 compromise bill provided $75 million in bilateral funds and $5 million in multilateral funds.

Global Fund to Fight AIDS, Tuberculosis and Malaria

The AIDS pandemic is still raging, two million people are dying every year of tuberculosis, and malaria kills one million a year, most of them children. One thing that would make a big difference in saving lives is to secure more resources for the new Global Fund to Fight AIDS, TB and Malaria (GFATM). The Fund is to provide needed medicines, other commodities, and basic services to those who need them most. RESULTS urged a 2001 supplemental appropriation of $1 billion for the GFATM. Sign-on letters to the President were initiated in both houses of Congress, urging him to take the lead. The Senate letter, initiated by Senator Leahy (D-VT), called for a $1.2 billion investment ($1 billion for the Global Health Fund and $200 million for USAID). The House letter, initiated by Representatives Barbara Lee (D-CA), Jim Leach (R-IA), and others, called for a $1 billion investment for the Fund. Although over 70 Representatives signed on, we were not successful in getting the supplemental funding in 2001. However, Congress did approve $250-300 million for the GFATM in 2002 spending bills.

In October, RESULTS sponsored a very successful news media conference call to urge increased resources to fight AIDS, TB and malaria. One of the guest speakers was the health minister of Pakistan. This event led to editorials in several newspapers including the Los Angeles Times, Boston Globe, Arizona Daily Star, Philadelphia Inquirer, and San Antonio Express News.

(And more…)

Mission Statement

RESULTS is a nonprofit, grassroots citizens' lobby working to create the political will to end hunger and the worst aspects of poverty.

We're committed to causing breakthroughs for people in realizing their own personal and political power.

RESULTS identifies sustainable solutions to the problems of hunger and poverty in the United States and around the world and works to generate the resources necessary to make them succeed.

What Other People Say About RESULTS

"RESULTS provides a roadmap for global involvement in planning for a better future"
Jimmy Carter

"You (your volunteers) are really the heart and soul, not only of RESULTS, but of reclaiming our democracy in this country and many others...What you are doing by the example you set goes far beyond even the programs and issues you are committed to, because you are symbolizing what we need to rekindle around the world."
Sen. Hillary
Rodham-Clinton
(D-New York)

"Pound for pound, RESULTS is the most effective lobby in Washington."
Rep. Tony Hall
(D—Ohio)

"I can never say enough good things about the work that you all do. It's always refreshing to work with people with such optimism and willingness to fight for what is right."
Rep. Sherwood
Boehlert
(R-New York)

"It is absolutely essential that citizens all across this country be part of an effort, like RESULTS, that reminds members of Congress why it is so important to invest in women and children...If members of RESULTS aren't talking about it, we won't hear about it."
Sen. Patty Murray
(D-Washington)

Get plugged in!
Participate in a RESULTS group near you!

There are active RESULTS groups in over 100 communities all over the country, **as well as individual activists in many other communities. The best way to get a feel for RESULTS and how we impact the world is by seeing us in action—come to a meeting near you and get involved locally.**

To get in contact with a local group, contact RESULTS at groups@resultsusa.org or call the RESULTS office at (202) 783-7100. Here is a listing of places where we currently have groups and whether they focus primarily on Domestic or Global poverty.

What We Mean By
POLITICAL WILL

At RESULTS, we talk a lot about Creating the Political Will to End Hunger. That could mean a lot of different things.

Political will is not simply about convincing politicians to pass laws that we favor. That may be the least of it, or at the least, the *result* of political will.

Political Will occurs when a majority of people decide that something is important, and refuse to lower standards or compromise principles when resolving the issues at hand.

And, Political Will is ultimately expressed in social and cultural values, mores, responsibilities, traditions and law.

We believe that...

- **Educating people about the issues of hunger and poverty**

- **Supporting people in taking actions consistent with their beliefs**

Training them to do it in a way that is effective and makes a difference
...will create the political will to end hunger and poverty.

120.—SOCIAL INDICATORS
WWW.AG.IASTATE.EDU/CENTERS/RDEV/
INDICATORS/ENTRY2.HTML

From INTRODUCTION on the website:

This annotated bibliography by Stephen Gasteyer and Cornelia Butler Flora is the first product of a cooperative agreement between the United States Environmental Protection Agency (EPA) and the North Central Regional Center for Rural Development (NCRCRD). The goal of this agreement is to examine and promote community and watershed indicators of environmental quality and social well-being. Our hope is that this product will help identify social indicators that will be of use to communities, government agents and others in locally-based initiatives to conserve, protect and enhance watershed and water quality.

Those involved in issues of water quality have increasingly come to realize that citizens need to lead in the protection of drinking water and other water resources. Through processes that will be explained below, social movements are forming around the United States to monitor water quality. Government agencies are using catchwords such as "partnership" and "participation" as key parts of their strategies for protecting the nation's water. Local water quality associations should be the groups with which government works. Those who do the work with water quality are well versed in the literature regarding the environmental indicators that help to guide citizen action, government action and policy. However, they often know little about the social indicators that tell us about citizen organizations themselves. What are the key contextual issues in the formation of a water quality association? What kinds of activities are important to maintain the sustainability of the association? How do we know if the association is successful? Social indicators can help us answer these questions. They can help us understand why environmental organizations must consider issues of social justice, poverty, equity and civic participation within a particular community.

Although social indicators have been compiled since methods of computation became sophisticated enough to try to measure the human condition (some say as early as the 1600s), our review of social indicators dates back to 1960. It was in this year that the President's Commission on National Goals submitted their report, Goals for Americans, to President Eisenhower (#34). This report, researched and written with private monies, provided a major overview of the status of Americans as they entered the 1960s and presented possibilities for moving beyond the problems of inequities in wealth and government services among ethnic and social groups. It called for more organized government efforts to track and respond to social developments in the United States.

Soon afterwards, government programs began debating how they might develop a social report that would mimic the economic reports on the state of the nation. Through the 1960s and 1970s, interest in being able to better collect and analyze data on social conditions grew in the bureaucracies of the U.S. and other governments. As the field developed, so did the number of areas where social indicators were deemed important. Community health and quality of life were added to the provision and availability of social services. Researchers began to link indicators of environmental quality and social indicators such as health.

This annotated bibliography is not intended to provide a comprehensive review of all social indicator sources produced during this 40-year span. We sought sources that would be of value to those interested in using indicators to help facilitate wise community management and development. The sources cited here should be useful in providing background resources on social indicators, as well as tools and indicators for use in communities. With this in mind, we have listed the indicator categories in our annotations so that people interested in finding new ideas for indicators can use our product as a resource. We have strayed from the strictly defined social indicator literature to include some of the important literature about sustainable communities, healthy communities and healthy ecosystems (including humans)—although we focus on that body of literature that either explicitly deals with indicators of social well-being or the interaction between social well-being and ecosystem quality. We have also included annotations of web sites, both on social indicators and sustainable communities.

121.—The State of World Population 2001
http://www.unfpa.org/swp/2001/ english/ch01.html#1

From the website:

Introduction

Over three and a half million years ago, two of modern humanity's ancestors left their footprints in the sand near what is now Laetoli in the United Republic of Tanzania. This couple was walking barefoot along a plain. Their people probably numbered in the hundreds or thousands and possessed very rudimentary implements. Only a remarkable chain of coincidences preserved their trail for our current inspection and wonder.

Today the footprints of humanity are impossible to miss. Human activity has affected every part of the planet, no matter how remote, and every ecosystem, from the simplest to the most complex. Our choices and interventions have transformed the natural world, posing both great possibilities and extreme dangers for the quality and sustainability of our civilizations, and for the intricate balances of nature.

Our numbers have doubled since 1960 to 6.1 billion, with growth mostly in poorer countries. Consumption expenditures have more than doubled since 1970, with increases mostly in richer countries. During this time, we have created wealth on an unimaginable scale, yet half the world still exists on less than $2 a day. We have learned how to extract resources for our use, but not how to deal with the resulting waste: emissions of carbon dioxide, for example, grew 12 times between 1900 and 2000. In the process we are changing the world's climate.

The great questions for the 21st century are whether the activities of the 20th century have set us on a collision course with the environment, and if so, what can we do about it? Human ingenuity has brought us this far. How can we apply it to the future so as to ensure the well-being of human populations, and still protect the natural world?

The stewardship of the planet and the well-being of its people are a collective responsibility. Everywhere we face critical decisions. Some are about how to protect and promote fundamental values such as the right to health and human dignity. Others reflect trade-offs between available options, or the desire to broaden the range of choice. We need to think carefully but urgently about what the choices are, and to take every action that will broaden choices and extend the time in which to understand their implications.

Today every part of the natural and human world is linked to every other. Local decisions have a global impact. Global policy, or the lack of it, affects local communities and the conditions in which they live. Humans have always changed and been changed by the natural world; the prospects for human development now depend on our wisdom in managing the relationship.

One of the key factors will be population. It is also one of the areas where action to broaden choices is universally available, affordable and agreed upon.

At this location on the web site:
http://www.unfpa.org/swp/2001/english/indicators/
indicators1.html

There is a table showing several key indicators of mortality, education and health for essentially all the countries of the planet.

Infant Mortality Rate (deaths during first year per 1,000 live births)
Life Expectancy
HIV Prevalence rate

And more…

122.—THE WORLDWATCH INSTITUTE— HTTP://WWW.WORLDWATCH.ORG

This is one organization dedicated to "keeping an eye on things".

From the web site:

Welcome to the Worldwatch Institute Online

Worldwatch is a non profit public policy research organization dedicated to informing policymakers and the public about emerging global problems and trends and the complex links between the world economy and its environmental support systems.

Worldwatch Institute Mission

The Worldwatch Institute is an independent research organization that works for an environmentally sustainable and socially just society, in which the needs of all people are met without threatening the health of the natural environment or the well-being of future generations. By providing compelling, accessible, and fact-based analysis of critical global issues, Worldwatch informs people around the world about the complex interactions between people, nature, and economies. Worldwatch focuses on the underlying causes of and practical solutions to the world's problems, in order to inspire people to demand new policies, investment patterns and lifestyle choices.

State of the World 2003

Building a world where we meet our own needs without denying future generations a healthy society is not impossible, but the challenge is to mobilize governments, businesses, and civil society to construct economies that are healthy for both people and the planet, reports State of the World 2003. According to the 20th anniversary edition of the Worldwatch Institute's award-winning report, scaling up recent successes in curbing infection, increasing the income of the poor, and advancing the use of renewable energy, among others, would soon put the world's economy on a more sustainable path.

123.—OPERATING SYSTEM EARTH— WWW.OSEARTH.COM

This web site is continually being updated. Check out the worldometers that show the population up to the second and other measures. The worlometers are at:

http://www.osearth.com/resources/worldometers/index.shtml

From the web site:

o.s.EARTH, Inc. (OSE) is a corporation established to acquire and commercialize the assets of the World Game Institute (WGI), a non-profit research and education organization. OSE provides experiential, simulation-based learning and training about world resources and issues. Its flagship product, developed by WGI over a ten-year period, is the Global Simulation Workshop. More than 2,000 clients from high schools to Fortune 500 corporations have included the WGI workshop in their educational and training programs. This game has reached nearly 250,000 participants in 48 U.S. states and 35 countries, and continues to improve and expand.

The World Game Institute
The World Game Institute was founded in 1972 by OSE principals Howard Brown and Medard Gabel in collaboration with renowned philosopher and designer, R. Buckminster Fuller. Fuller foresaw the need for a great World Peace Game as an alternative to War Games, and saw the goal of the World Game as making "the world work for 100% of humanity, in the shortest possible time, through spontaneous cooperation, and without ecological offense or the disadvantage of anyone." o.s.EARTH purchased many of the WGI's principal assets in 2000.

124.—CONCLUSION/SUMMARY

If you have read all 123 items collected here for potential participation, you have done more that I thought you might. If you have found a few of the 123 items that have stirred you into action I'm delighted. If you have perused the book in a way that has you creating your own participation in having the world work I congratulate you. In any case, I sincerely desire that you have looked at the question below and have come up with an answer for yourself. I wish you well!

"So, What are _You_ Going to do about it?"

0-595-26472-7

www.ingramcontent.com/pod-product-compliance
Lightning Source LLC
Chambersburg PA
CBHW032058280526
45784CB00012B/30